JOY ROBERTSON

BROKEN Covenant

A FAMILY IN CRISIS

AUCTOREM
HOUSE

Auctorem House
276 5th Ave, Ste 704-2591
New York, NY 10001
www.auctoremhouse.com
1.888.332.7718

Vector art by Freepik

ACKNOWLEDGEMENT

I would like to thank the family of Calvary Life Center, for their love and encouragement over the years. You have played such a vital part in my growth as a Christian. My children and I could not have made it through those difficult times without your love. Thanks also to my friends Jerry and Louise Pietrorazio for showing me daily what it means to be Christ like.

To my Bishop, the Reverend Fredrick Dibble Sr., words cannot express my gratitude for your guidance over the years. Only when we get to Heaven will you know the difference you have made in my life and the lives of my children.

To my children, Nicole and Jordan, thank you for encouraging me to complete this project. Nicole, thank you for working tirelessly in the editing of this book. I am most proud to be called your mother. Know that the promise of God's word was more than enough to see us through.

Joy

arch 3, 1999 is a day I'll not likely forget. The events of that day are forever chiseled in my memory: it was my D-Day. My husband Ros had been going through a series of tests for reoccurring pain on his right side. There were numerous tests: X-rays, CAT scans, blood work, and several biopsies that came back either negative or inconclusive. He had a request from his physician to do one last test, which is what brings me to this day.

March 3, 1999 was a Wednesday: my day off from the bank where I worked. It was a day for laundry, house cleaning, and various other tasks that come with being a wife and mother. A typical day off from work consisted of getting breakfast and lunch ready for Ros in order to get him off to work then driving our eighteen- year-old daughter Nicole to school in another town since there was no bus she could take as a result of where we lived. Afterwards, I'd rush home to wait for my eight-year-old son's bus to arrive... it was only after Jordan's bus drove off that my day really began with the household chores and preparation of meals that needed to be finished before everyone came back home in the evening so we could get ready for the weekly Wednesday night bible study at the church we attended.

To say I loved my family would be an understatement: I had two beautiful children, and even though there was quite a disparity in their ages, Jordan clearly adored his big sister who, at the time, was applying to college. We were all looking forward to the college tours and seeing where she would spend the next four years of her life. If that weren't enough, I had a wonderful husband who loved me in a way that I had never experienced love before. I came from a single parent household, so to have that family unit was an amazing accomplishment to me, and I cherished every moment of it.

In the midst of going up the stairs from the laundry room with a load I had just completed, I heard the garage door open. I found it unusual that Ros would be home in the middle of the afternoon: he normally got up at three or four o'clock in the morning to study for the ministry. He was getting a degree in theology from Christian Life College, and it was his custom to be up at 3:00 a.m. to study before leaving for his engineering job at Exmet Corporation. He found it difficult to study after work, so this routine worked well for him. Since he would leave the house at about six o'clock in the morning, and work until seven or eight in the evening, it was quite unusual for him to be home at 2:30 in the afternoon.

As I continued up the stairs, I asked the question aloud, "Why are you home so early?" There was no response. I assumed he hadn't heard me, so I repeated the question. I kept asking with no response. Since I thought he just did not hear me, I went on folding clothes. When Ros finally made his way up the stairs from the garage, I heard him calling for me to come into the living room. I told him I would be there in a minute, but he insisted, "Honey, come to the living room now." His tone was more abrupt than usual. I walked into the living room, asking again how it was that he was home so early, but the face I saw when I entered the living room was not the face of my husband. The very life had gone out of him as if someone had given him a death sentence... and so it was.

My husband had a wonderful smile. I believe I fell in love with him because of that smile. Whenever he smiled, the room took on a different appearance, and that smile always seemed to make everything better so that no matter how angry I was with him, he would smile his way through as if nothing happened, making me forget why I was mad with him in the first place. But on that day in March, there was no smile. The room grew darker as the moments passed... then after what seemed like an eternity, he declared that the doctor had called him at work to tell him the results had come back from the last set of tests: they were positive. Cancer was the word of the day, and I believe he called it the Big C. I had no concept of what the Big C was, so I had to ask... and in that moment, I was so sorry that I had. I don't recall much more of that moment, but I do remember holding him very tightly, as if by holding him tightly it would all go away.

After recovering from the initial shock, I put on my "fixable" hat. This was big, but in my mind, it was fixable. In my mind, if there was a problem, there had to be a solution; and once we found the solution, we could fix the problem and move on. I remember putting dinner on the table later that day and saying to him, "This is going to be fine." We went to Wednesday night Bible study and told our pastor because we wanted him to pray with us and believe for a miracle.

Thus began the ten-month journey of the covenant that would be broken, ft is amazing how quickly one's world can shatter and how very fragile this life that we hold so tightly to can be. Only six months before that life-changing day, Ros had been given a clean bill of health from his yearly physical. I recall that apart from the small cyst on his butt cheek which the doctor removed right there in the office, he was in excellent health. According to him, he would be around for a very long time, and so I took that as confirmation that we would have a long life together as man and wife. So how do we go from perfect health to a death sentence in only six months? That must have been the question of the decade.

Now, there we were on March 4, 1999 in Dr. Frank Alfano's office, discussing what options, if any, we had in this fight against hepatocellular carcinoma. Dr. Alfano was quite sympathetic toward my husband and told him, "If you were my brother, I would be telling you the same thing: fight this thing on every level." He told us there were great strides taking place at Memorial Sloan Kettering Cancer Center in New York City, and that this would be a good place to start. Unfortunately, our insurance company would not allow us to go out of our network. This meant that we wouldn't be allowed to go to another state's facilities without first going through the services offered in our state. If we were not successful in receiving the services we needed or if our facilities did not offer the treatments needed to combat this particular illness, then we could get a referral from our personal physician for services beyond our state's borders, but only after exhausting every possibility within the frame of our network. Dr. Alfano gave us a referral for Yale-New Haven Hospital. We had to wait two weeks before we could get an appointment with the doctor at Yale-New Haven, but the day finally came, and we were on our way.

One sunny afternoon, a few days before our trip to Yale-New Haven, Ros and I decided to take a walk. We had never really been big on walking before that day, so I'm not sure what prompted this particular stroll down our tree-lined street—maybe it was just a reflex of the reflective state of mind we found ourselves in since getting the news of this diagnosis. Either way, it seemed as good a time as any to enjoy the fresh spring air. After a relatively mild winter, the trees and plants took advantage of the unseasonably warm weather to start showing signs of new life. It's the miracle of the circle of life, really—in order for new life to spring up, something first had to die. It's easy to think about death and dying when it comes to nature and seasons; but when thoughts of dying hits closer to home, it's a bit harder to swallow.

"I'm going to beat this thing. God is going to heal me."

Ros' comment came seemingly out of the blue, as if he were respond-ing to my silent thoughts. There was an air of confidence in his voice, but looking deep in his eyes, I could see shreds of doubt, as if he made the statement to convince himself of the thought.

"And if God doesn't heal you?"

The question seemed to catch him off guard. After thinking about it for a bit, he said that he was ready if God somehow didn't see fit to cure him of this dreaded disease. Despite the conviction with which he spoke, though, I wasn't completely convinced. There was a look of reflection on his face as he thought about past memories and how he would miss me and the children if somehow this disease ended life as he knew it.

Later that week, we found ourselves at Yale-New Haven, waiting for our turn to see the doctor. The wait was painfully long, wondering what kind of news we'd get after it was all said and done. I'm sure the waiting would have felt even longer had our bishop and his wife not come with us. They played such an intricate role in our lives since we moved to the state of Connecticut from Quebec ten years prior. Fredrick Dibble, Sr. had been a father figure to both Ros and myself. Ros' father had long since passed away, and I hadn't seen my father who lived in London, England in many years. What a great blessing it was for us to have those who we considered family there with us to help us through that very difficult time. However, I did get the sense that the bishop's wife, a fellow squeamish person, was having the same thought I was: *I would rather be any place but here.* She and I are not hospital people. I have passed out in three different hospitals in two different countries, and by the flushed look on her face, I suspect that, had we been there any longer, she might have started a trend of her own.

Ros, the bishop, and I entered the doctor's office. Sister Dibble elected to stay in the waiting area for self-preservation purposes, I believe. Ros was asked to sit on a table as the doctor examined the CAT scan and MRI reports. Just the look on the doctor's face told me that this was not good. The words that left his lips were "inoperable." Then, Ros began to speak. One of the attributes I loved about my husband is that he did not always have to talk—I often thought of him as the strong, silent type. But in that moment, there was nothing silent about him as he was visibly upset.

"You're telling me that my life is over? I'm forty-five years old, and my life is over?"

I reached over to tell him to calm down.

"I don't want to calm down! He is telling me my life is over! No, I don't accept, I won't accept that. There has to be a mistake."

From the look on the doctor's face, there was no mistake. The doctor went on to explain, "Mr. Robertson, with the enormity of the tumors, I don't believe you would survive the surgery, and I'm not willing to take that chance."

I don't believe I had ever seen my husband cry in public before. In fact, I don't remember having seen him cry in any public forum, for that matter. He was always so reserved with his emotions... at his mother's funeral a few years back, I looked for some signs of unraveling in his character... he had so wanted me to meet her, and I never got the chance... I thought that bothered him more than anything, and yet, even then, he kept his emotions in check. Now, here we were in this stranger's office, and the tears flowed freely from his eyes. I doubt he even realized he was crying. My husband, so full of life with dreams and aspirations yet to be realized, was now given a death sentence, with CAT scans, MRI, X-rays, and blood tests confirming the grim reality—*inoperable.*

We left the doctor's office and took the elevator in absolute silence, the bishop and his wife went to their car while we walked across the parking lot to ours. The air in that underground parking lot smelled so different than when we first came in: the exhaust from the cars was more evident as if someone had left the parking lot in a hurry and flooded the engine of their car. The silence was so eerie that I felt my own heart pounding through my chest as if, at any moment, the walls of my chest would burst wide open, and if I didn't take a deep breath at that moment, there would be an explosion of emotions I would not be able to control. I took a quick look at Ros' face as we entered the car to see if I could get a sense of what he was feeling, but all I saw was a blank look, as if he had stepped into another dimension. I did not dare speak in that moment because, well, what is there to say when you hear the word *inoperable?*

The drive back to Waterbury from Yale normally took about thirty minutes; but that day, it felt three times as long. I thought stopping for lunch at TGI Fridays would take our minds off of the grim news we just heard. Fridays had long been our favorite place to have lunch in times past, but this day, it didn't have the same appeal. The meal tasted bland as if someone had thrown it together in a hurry, and the chatter around us was totally irrelevant to the moment we were in. With the check paid, we made our way back to the car and drove in silence once again, this time all the way home. The following day, we went back to Dr. Alfano to tell him the news from Yale and to see what other options we had. He made some phone calls and got us the referral we needed for Sloan Kettering, telling us not to give up. "They are doing great things there," I recall him saying. Once again, we were optimistic that maybe, just maybe, there would be a light at the end of this dark tunnel.

At 8:20 a.m. on April 2, 1999, we made the two-hour drive from Waterbury to Sloan Kettering in New York City to meet with Dr. Fong. He was a specialist in hepatocellular carcinoma, and we were told that, if anyone could help, it would be him. Our appointment was scheduled for 10:00 a.m., but we left early to avoid the traffic, and because we weren't exactly sure where the hospital was. Since Ros' pain in his side had become extremely uncomfortable at times, I had taken on the task of doing all the driving. I certainly was not happy about having to drive in New York City, but you do what needs to be done when it needs to be done. We arrived in the lobby of Sloan Kettering an hour and a half early. To say we were somewhat anxious would be an understatement. What we saw while we waited for Dr. Fong certainly didn't help. There was so much devastation from this monster called cancer. We saw people with facial parts missing, oxygen tanks being carried around, and people who were not only robbed of their ability to do the very basic for themselves but also robbed of their dignity. Unless you are thrown into this terrible reality, you have no idea how every day so many are fighting for their lives. As I sat there watching, I wondered what the percentage was of people who lost their lives to this disease every year. Would my family become a part of that statistic? It's amazing the thoughts that go through one's mind when there's too much time to think.

We met Dr. Fong and several other doctors who were brought in to assess the situation. Each one, we were told, was an expert in his or her field. As Dr. Fong began to read the X-rays we brought from Dr. Alfano, the look on his face was so transparent—I don't know if he was a poker player, but if he did play, I suspect he wasn't very good. The look on his face indicated that he was dissatisfied with the X-rays we brought, so he ordered new X-rays along with a new MRI, a new CAT scan, and numerous blood tests. Most of that day at Sloan was spent going from one department to another to be tested, scanned or examined, then waiting for one test result or another, as if one more test would change the situation or reveal something that we did not already know.

We took a break from all the morning's activities and went across the street for lunch. I thought it was appropriate that there was such a nice diner so close that one could go and escape from the world of cancer, even if it was only for lunch. When we returned to Sloan Kettering, Dr. Fong was waiting for us with some of the results from tests done earlier. He began, "The diagnosis is confirmed by the alpha-fetoprotein test. The normal count is fifteen; Mr. Robertson, your count is twenty-nine thousand." There are times when you can hide your emotions and let everyone believe that you are in control; then, there are times that before you realize or have a chance to collect yourself, your emotions crescendo, and everyone realizes you are gasping for air. That's where we found ourselves in that moment: gasping for every ounce of air that our lungs could get. I didn't understand what the alpha-fetoprotein test was all about, but I did understand the disparity between fifteen and twenty-nine thousand. Without missing a beat, Dr. Fong continued to speak, "I believe I can operate..."

"Did he say operate?"

Ros asked me the question as if we were not in the same room, hearing the very same thing that was being said.

"You can operate?"

His attention went to Dr. Fong as he repeated the question. For a moment, you would think there was an echo in the room as this question was repeated over and over again.

"Yes, I believe so."

And for the first time since this ordeal began, there was a smile on my husband's face. We had found a glimmer of hope as Dr. Fong set his plan to operate in motion. There would be another visit before the day of the operation for more tests, X-rays, MRIs, CAT scans, and blood tests. But this was okay because we had a shred of hope: he can operate. In a single moment, we had gone from *"inoperable"* to *"I believe I can operate.*" Surely, we could tolerate more tests if it meant that Ros' life could be spared. Hope indeed lived that day, and we were thankful; probably more thankful than we had ever been about anything before. We rode back to Connecticut in a better state of mind than when we had left. We sang and prayed all the way home, thanking the Lord for the little bit of hope we had received.

There was a renewed desire in me after that initial visit to Sloan. I decided that if there was a chance my family would come through this storm, then I had a role to play in that survival. The only weapon I had was prayer and the Bible. So I began putting up scriptures on the walls in the house. Scripture, I thought, would encourage not only me but Ros as well.

I shall not die, but live,
And declare the works of the Lord.
The Lord has chastened me severely,
But He has not given me over to death.

(Psalm 118: 17–18)

I will walk before the Lord in the land of the living.

(Psalm 116:9)

Oh, give thanks to the Lord, for He is good!
For His mercy endures forever.
The Lord is for me among those who help me;
Therefore I shall see my desire on those who hate me.
Lt is better to trust in the Lord
Than to put confidence in man.

(Psalm 118:1, 7–8)

I love the Lord, because He has heard
My voice and my supplications.
Because He has inclined His ear to me,
Therefore I will call upon Him as long as I live.

(Psalm 116:1–2)

This is the day the Lord has made;
We will rejoice and be glad in it.

(Psalm 118:24)

Remember the word to your servant,
Upon which You have caused me to hope.
This is my comfort in my affliction,
For Your word has given me life.

(Psalm 119:49, 50)

Those who trust in the Lord
Are like Mount Zion,
Which cannot be moved, but abides forever.
As the mountains surround Jerusalem,
So the Lord surrounds His people
From this time forth and forever.

(Psalm 125:1–2)

Out of the depths I have cried to You, O Lord;
Lord, hear my voice!
Let Your ears be attentive
To the voice of my supplications.

(Psalm 130:1–2)

It shall come to pass
That before they call, I will answer;
And while they are still speaking, I will hear.

(Isaiah 65:24)

Call to Me, and I will answer you, and show you great and mighty
things, which you do not know.

(Jeremiah 33:3)

There is no fear in love; but perfect love casts out fear, because
fear involves torment. But he who fears has not been made perfect
in love.

(1 John 4:18)

That your faith should not be in the wisdom of men but in the
power of God.

(1 Corinthians 2:5)

If the spirit of the ruler rises against you,
Do not leave your post;
For conciliation pacifies great offenses.

(Ecclesiastes 10:4)

Up until then, I thought of myself as a good Christian. I did all the right things. I was faithful to the church, I paid my tithes and showed up at all the prayer meetings and outreach programs. I even facilitated some of those programs. So if those were the things that made one a good Christian, then I would say that I was a good Christian. But letting the Word of God become a part of my life—now *that* was new. As I began to post these scriptures, they came alive to me. For the first time, I realized that they were more than mere words; their presence was speaking comfort to my soul. Were it not for those scriptures, I would have lost all hope. As Hebrews 4:12 says: *For the word of God is living and powerful, and sharper than any two- edged sword, piercing even to the division of soul and spirit, and of joints and marrow, and is a discerner of the thoughts and intents of the heart.*

It dawned on me that these scriptures were more for me than they were for Ros. I would need them if I were to survive the winds of this storm.

Unfortunately, I was not the only person who would need to survive the winds of this storm. I hadn't told Nicole and Jordan about their father's illness, and it was clear that Ros could not bring himself to tell them, either. I mean, how do you tell your own children that you're dying? In my mind, these children were so precious that anything I could do to protect them from painful news was a necessary measure. For as long as I could, I did my job as a mother and made sure to keep this dreaded secret. Every day, I tried hard to pretend there was nothing wrong. But when I was alone, thoughts of this eventuality flooded my mind. How would I make it if I should find myself alone, having to take care of two children? How would I make it in life without Ros? We only made plans as a couple. Never did we conceive a possible solo flight in *our* plan. But there we were, having to face this possibility.

As I was trying to keep our family unit from being torn apart, we received an unexpected phone call—it was Ros' older sister in Montreal. They hadn't spoken in years, but when she heard he was ill, she felt it necessary to call and see if there was anything she could do. I suppose that was a blessing because they had a chance to talk and clear up a riff they had between them for quite some time. Ros spoke often about his older sister and how he wished they could have the relationship they once had when he was a child. She had been a second mother to him when he was younger, even going as far as sponsoring him to migrate to Canada from Jamaica, ensuring he went to a good school, and basically acting as his guardian until a dispute separated them for a number of years...that is, until she heard he was sick. Knowing how important family is to Ros and knowing how much he missed his sister, it was heartening to see that this illness caused them to reunite.

We went to Sloan for a second time to go over the procedures for the upcoming surgery. Appointments were set for another X-ray, blood tests, and another CAT scan because the tumors had grown since the previous tests. Our bishop graciously offered to go with us, and I can't tell you how glad I was that someone else would be there. Sometimes, it helps to know that someone else is there even if there is nothing they themselves can do to make the situation better. Just having him along for the ride lifted our spirits. We made the journey from Connecticut to New York once again. While stuck in traffic in Lower Manhattan, I decided to call Dr. Fong's office just to let him know that we were running late. To my surprise, I was told that the doctor was not in his office. Not only was he not in his office, he was out of the country at a medical conference and would not be back for another two weeks! We would have to reschedule. I heard myself saying to the secretary, "Do you realize we don't live in this city? We drove all the way from Connecticut, and no one bothered to call us to let us know that we would have to reschedule, even though we had a scheduled appointment?" Her response to me was, "I'm sorry; it can't be helped."

"Well, of course, it can be helped!" I heard myself saying. "Someone whose brain cells were actually working could have picked up the phone and dialed the Robertsons to say, 'I'm sorry; the doctor will have to reschedule your appointment because he will be out of the country for a medical conference, so there is no need to drive all the way to New York City only to be told that you will have to reschedule.' So, yes, it can be helped!"

I don't believe my bishop had ever seen that side of me before. I felt the blood of anger flood my face as I spoke on the phone to the secretary. Much of that anger stemmed from the fact that, by this time, the evidence of cancer was visible in Ros' body. He had lost weight and could no longer hide the pain that was now frequent and more intense. Every moment the surgery was delayed, was a moment that was lost to him.

We drove back to Connecticut in complete silence. I believe everyone in the car was afraid to speak. My own anger was still raging, though silently. That secretary being sorry was of absolutely no help to us. This crisis seemed not to matter to anyone else but those of us who were caught in it. Finally, the bishop broke the silence. That was the first time he gave us the scriptures about our faith being not in the wisdom of men but in the power of the Almighty and about God's perfect love casting out all our fears.

We decided that Wednesday night that I would take the children to Bible study since the day's trip had left Ros weary. Fatigue came on so easily in those days, ft seemed so unreal that this man who normally worked fifteen hours a day after getting up to study at four or five in the morning suddenly had no energy to make it to the place he loved to go more than anything, ft felt like something was playing a cruel joke on us, and we were the only ones not laughing.

I drove the children to church that evening, and as I waited at the stop sign for the cars to go by, I heard a voice say, "Mom, what's wrong?" It's as if I was lost in a nightmare; I know I heard someone speaking, but it took me a moment to realize it was my daughter Nikki.

"Whafs wrong? You're crying..."

"Crying?"

"Yes; you're crying."

I hadn't even realized that the heat on my face was actually from tears. I could no longer keep this dreaded secret. The dam was broken, and once a dam is broken, there is no containing the flood. So, I pulled the car over and began to explain to my children the reason for my tears. When I was done, I heard a small voice in the back of the car saying, "Don't worry, Mommy; I'll take care of you!" ft was my eight-year-old son, Jordan. He had the insight and wisdom to empathize with me in that moment, ft is absolutely amazing how at times we as parents underestimate the intelligence of our children when in fact they have so much more understanding and insight than we give them credit for. So now, with the secret being revealed, I no longer had to manage my emotions.

*I*t wasn't until early May that we finally got the call to reschedule the appointment that was interrupted by the good doctor's out-of-country medical conference. On the first Thursday in May, we met with Dr. Fong and his team in a conference room at Sloan Kettering to go over the procedure that would take place. Once again, more blood tests and scans; X-rays had to be taken before we could proceed. Dr. Fong explained to us that at that point, the embolization process would be the best way to proceed with this type of cancer. A small incision would be made in Ros' chest just below the rib cage, and a scope would be inserted to blast the tumors, breaking them up into smaller pieces. That would make it easier for the surgeons to operate: they would remove the blasted pieces and then pair away at the liver itself to remove the scarred liver tissue resulting from the disease. This would give the liver a chance to repair itself with medication and time. While we waited for the embolization appointment date, close friends of ours came to visit us from Canada. I have known Elvis and his wife, Sonia, since we were all teenagers growing up in Montreal; and when I met Ros, he and Elvis became more like brothers than friends. They helped us make the transition from Montreal to Connecticut, and we in turn helped them move from Montreal to Ottawa. When they heard that Ros was ill, they made the seven-hour drive to be with us for support. We took a trip to Mystic Seaport to show them around and also to get our minds off the upcoming surgery. Sonia and I went shopping while the men went about doing whatever men do. It was a wonderful weekend—for a few days, I forgot about the fact that my husband was sick, with the exception of the times when a look of distress on Ros' face reminded me it was time to give him his medication. I had come to understand the look of distress on his face meant that he was in more pain than he wanted anyone to know. But for a few days, not even those moments could stop us from just being two couples having a good time, reminiscing about the friendships we had discovered years before and praying that we would be friends for many more years to come.

Of course, all good things have their ending, and the end of this weekend getaway brought us right back to Sloan Kettering's door. Being forewarned that we were in for a time-consuming process, May 14 found Ros and I making that all-too-familiar journey from Waterbury to New York City. We made plans to meet two of his sisters. His older sister had come down from Canada, and another sister lived in New York. Meeting at Sloan Kettering at 6:30 a.m., we took time to pray together before the embolization, which was scheduled for 9:30 a.m. At 9:30 on the dot, my husband was prepped and ready for surgery. One of the nurses instructed me and Ros' sisters to go up to the recovery room where they would bring him after the procedure. We took what seemed to be a long journey up the elevator to his recovery room. We didn't have to wait long though because in less than an hour, Ros was being wheeled into to the room. Immediately, I knew things could not have gone as intended. A few minutes later, Dr. Fong walked in the room followed by his entourage, declaring that the tumors were too many and too big for the embolization process. Instead, they would have to try opening up his stomach to remove the tumors—that would require a six- to seven-hour operation. The only thought I had was: "What will I tell him when he wakes up?" For the next hour or so, his sisters and I came up with many different scenarios, except none of them really made sense to us. And if we ourselves were not convinced, how could we possibly convince him? One of the problems with telling a lie is that you always have to remember exactly what the lie is.

When the anesthetic wore off and he finally woke up, he looked right at me and said, "It didn't work, did it?"

"No," I said, trying my best to sound positive...but the doctor thinks another procedure will work better in your case."

That was as unconvincing a statement as any I have ever made.

We made another appointment with Dr. Fong's nurse for the six-to seven-hour surgery where the surgeons would open Ros' stomach completely and cut away at the tumors. Dr. Fong remained optimistic, but in our minds, the psychological damage was already done. We came back from Sloan that day more dejected than ever. When we finally made it home that Friday night, we were both physically and emotionally exhausted. Ros began to feel discomfort from the incision, and my heart hurt from the sting of the failed surgery. I gave Ros some medication for his discomfort, but there was nothing I could take for the pain in my heart. I felt an over-whelming desire to go to the church. We lived only few minutes away from the sanctuary, and as I walked in the door, I felt a sudden sense of despair but knew that was where I needed to be at that time. It felt as if an old friend was there waiting for me, a friend who would understand everything I had been through that day... so I stayed awhile and began to commune with this old friend. As I talked to Him, I poured out everything that was in my heart: I cried, I complained... I made a strong case about what a good person I thought I was or was trying to be... I made it clear how it was not fair that cancer should be a part of our lives, and I wanted to know what my old friend was going to do to help me. In that moment, there was a sense of warmth that engulfed me, like someone wrapped me in a warm blanket. Before I knew it, time was far spent; when I looked at the clock, it was midnight... then midnight turned to morning... I suppose there were those who were looking for me from midnight to dawn, several people came in the sanctuary; but when they realized where I was, most left me alone in my lament. Some people stayed awhile, leading to an impromptu prayer meeting that lasted until the following morning when those who were coming in for our Greater Anointing Prayer meeting, or GAP, streamed through the door. The love that filled the room that morning was as close to the love of God as I had ever felt, ft overwhelmed me and Ros, who had since joined that impromptu prayer meeting. I did not hear when he came in, but I eventually recognized his distinct Jamaican accent whitewashed with a slight American twang; and when he spoke in the language that only Heaven could comprehend, there was no mistaking that he had stepped into another dimension. That morning, I realized that my relationship with the Lord Jesus Christ was different—it could not be the same because when my circumstances caused me to doubt His everlasting love, He used that same circumstance to show me how much He loved us. I had spent the night with Emmanuel [*GOD with us*]. As paradoxical as it all seemed, it was never more evident than in that darkest time of our lives that we were loved with an everlasting love... it is impossible to explain the intimate presence of God that filled the sanctuary on that Friday... the best way to describe it is to say that every kind of love remotely imaginable was in that sanctuary all at once: the intimate love of a husband for his wife, the tender love of a mother for her children, the strong love of brothers one for another, the selfless love of a soldier laying down his life for his country... it was all there and more, all wrapped up in the everlasting love of the Savior for His children; we being the privileged benefactors of this experience in spite of—or even because of—our circumstance, which had in no way changed His everlasting love toward us.

A few days after that Friday night encounter, Ros attended a board meeting at church. I was so excited that he was able to go: at this point, his energy level was so low that it took all he had just to make it to the car. So when, on this occasion, he insisted on driving himself to the meeting, I didn't object, not wanting to take away what little ounce of independence he had left. Less than an hour after he left home, however, our friend Jerry had to bring him back home. He was in excruciating pain, and the moment they walked in, any optimism I mustered from his solo excursion blew out the door. I held him in my arms that night and sang these words:

> *In Christ alone, I place my trust*
> *And find my glory in the power of the cross.*
> *In every victory, let it be said of me*
> *My source of strength, my source of hope Is Christ Alone.*

As we waited for the ambulance, I thought about how many nights we would have to spend in the hospital before this would all be over. The prospect of spending the night in the hospital was not appealing to me at all... how I had come to despise that word—*hospital*—it was a place where sick people should go to receive help, but for us, it had become a place of absolute torment, knowing that there was seemingly nothing the doctors or nurses there could do. I was glad when our bishop came to our rescue once again and stayed with us in that sterile room. He prayed for God to give us peace that night... Because he was a man of unshakeable faith, I believed every word he prayed. I knew Heaven had answered because the mood in that hospital room was visibly lighter. Even with Ros on a constant drip of morphine all night, we were able to joke with him about not getting too comfortable with being under the influence of drugs.

The bishop's presence made such a difference in that room that night, but when we left the hospital, there was much to contend with: we tried acupuncture to alleviate the increasing pain Ros was feeling since morphine alone was no longer doing the job. We were desperate to find something to bring him some comfort as the pain grew to unbearable levels. It's amazing what you'll consider when you're desperate: I received a phone call from a Mr. Mario Soto (someone had given him our phone number) who wanted us to travel to Mexico to try some experimental treatment that included taking aloe vera juice, shark oil, colloidal silver, syner zine, and enzokire, all for only $10,900. In the midst of getting this offer, we were still waiting on Sloan Kettering to see when Ros' operation would take place. We consulted with Dr. Fong about the experimental treatment—he made it clear that if we went ahead with the experimental treatment, the operation would not be scheduled because there was no predicting what all those elements would do to Ros' body. There we were, caught between the proverbial rock and a hard place: do we take a chance on this experimental treatment or do we wait on Sloan? The weight of making such a decision weighed heavily on both of us: how were we going to choose one procedure over another? What happened if we made the wrong choice? Whatever we decided, there would be no going back: Ros' life weighed in the balance. The experimental treatment was just that: an experiment. Could I trust the life of my husband—my soul mate—to a mere experiment? After spending restless nights agonizing over the decision, we eventually chose to stick with Sloan Kettering since they had previous success in treating hepatocellular carcinoma; in the meantime, though, it was easy to see Ros' features were taking on a different appearance: his stomach was now protruding, and his eyes looked gauntly, as if his body was starving in one area and overfed in another. I was always careful not to show my emotions in front of him, but as I walked into the bedroom one night, I started to realize the magnitude of what was taking place. Moving slowly over to the side of the bed where Ros was laying, I kneeled down to have a word of prayer with him since I heard him moaning from the other room. As I laid my hands on his stomach for the first time in a long time, I could feel that his entire stomach was as hard as rocks. In that moment, I knew this situation would not end well; and before I realized it, warm tears flushed my face. There was no place to hide this time; as I knelt at his bed in silence, no words were spoken, but that night, I reconciled myself to the fact that he would not recover from this illness... we both understood at that moment how unfair life could be. No matter how much we try to convince ourselves otherwise, it doesn't matter how good we think we are or how well we believe we have lived: when the rain falls, everyone gets wet. And this was our downpour.

hile we waited for a preadmission test to Sloan for the surgery to cut down Ros' liver, Dr. Alfano gave us a referral to Mount Sinai for a possible liver transplant. There were three appointments in that one day: a 10:00 a.m. meeting with Dr. Segal and his team for interviews and evaluation to see if Ros would qualify for a transplant, a 12:00 p.m. meeting with the social worker and her team to discuss the different aspects of care we would have to look forward to if a transplant were to take place, followed by a 1:30 p.m. appointment for another CAT scan. The last CAT scan was very difficult—it had become quite apparent that Ros' liver was not functioning at full capacity. His appetite had decreased dramatically with the growth of the tumors, and with time, it became more difficult to hold much of anything down. He made it clear to the nurse that he would not be able to drink all the liquid she gave him before the exam, but she insisted that he drink it all, or she would not be able to do the test. She soon found out that when a patient says he can't do something, she should perhaps take his word for it: after all, who better than the patient to know what he or she can and cannot do? Maybe next time, she won't have to clean up the floor.

After meeting with the social worker and Dr. Segal's team, it seemed unlikely that a transplant would take place based on several reasons: one, it was discovered through one of the blood tests that Ros had hepatitis B. During the interview, Dr. Segal told us in no uncertain terms that Mt. Sinai would not give a good liver to someone who had hepatitis B because, in their eyes, it would be asking them to waste a liver. Even so, after having gone through the whole informational process for the transplant, we found out that there was a two-year waiting period for the list. Anyone looking at Ros could see from his physical appearance that he did not have two years to wait, so the only other option was to find a donor on our own.

So the task began: how do you ask someone to donate a part of his or her body to try and save your life? There was no question in my mind that if our blood types were compatible, I would be the donor. I was ready to do any and everything if there was even a slight possibility of saving Ros' life. Of course, Ros would hear nothing of it, saying that one of us had to be here for the children in case things did not go well for him. He was quite adamant about that, so we made the decision instead to call his nephew in Georgia and ask if he would be willing to donate a portion of his liver. Dane was young and in extremely good health, so he would have a better chance of coming through the operation with less adverse effects than someone who was not in the best of health.

Dane came up from Georgia for the family meeting. As we went through the process of learning what would be required, Dane's only concern at the time was that we would take care of his family while he was unable to. For us, that went without saying, if he was willing to put his own life on the line (which I thought was a remarkable thing for anyone to do), the least we could do was take care of his family.

The act of asking his nephew to give a part of his body to save his life weighed heavily on Ros. You could see it on his face. There are times when we can't hide the depths of what we are feeling... every emotion was evident on his face... even with the heaviness of asking Dane to make that enormous sacrifice, arrangements were made to have Dane's blood type tested to see if the two were a match. Though he had consented to give Ros a portion of his liver, if their blood types were not compatible, it would all be for nothing and we would be right back where we started.

Following the family meeting, Dane went back to Georgia, and a second meeting was set for him to go to the hospital to be tested. As his nephew drove away from the house that day, a scripture came to mind: "No greater love has a man than this: that he would lay down his life for his friend" (John 15:13 [KJV]). My mind took me back to only a few years before this illness when this same nephew had found himself in a difficult situation in North Carolina: he was in an automobile with someone who was transporting illegal substances; and when the police pulled the car over, everyone inside was arrested. Ros drove all night long to help secure his nephew's safety. His nephew was all too grateful to return the favor...

Everything changed, though, with that second trip to the emergency room. It seemed that while the doctors were waiting to decide what course of action to take, the tumors were growing by leaps and bounds. We spent another night in the emergency room... this clearly was becoming a trend I could not get used to. Several of the saints from our church came to see how we were doing—some stayed awhile while others popped their heads in the hospital room just to say hello. My guess is that some just came by to make sure Ros was still among the land of the living since word had gone out that he had taken a turn for the worst. I suppose some came out of curiosity to see what "the worst" was, while others had a genuine desire to make sure we were all right. Diana O'Neal was one of those genuine saints: she had adopted me and Ros when we first moved to Connecticut and oh, how we loved her—I believe the feeling was mutual. I remember her concern for me when she thought I looked flushed in that hospital room. She asked the nurse if it would be okay for me to use the empty hospital bed to lay down then proceeded to get me something to drink. I was most thankful for Diana who I've called mother since; even though she did not give birth to me, over the years, she has certainly treated me as if I was one of her own.

It was now late in May, and we were still waiting to get a definite date as to when they would try to operate a second time. Dr. Fong hoped this next procedure would work since the embolization idea was a failure. Once again, we went back to Sloan Kettering, where Dr. Fong's nurse finally set a date for the second operation, which included removing two-thirds of the liver after which Ros would undergo a long process of recovery... if he survived. I began to make preparations for the children during our time away at the hospital. Though there were several people in our church I could leave them with, I wanted them to stay in their own home and sleep in their own beds. It was bad enough for us as parents that we were going to be away from them for an unspecified amount of time; the least we could do was make things as normal for them as possible. I asked my friend Ruby Tenor if she could stay with the children at our house. I explained to her that I wanted them to stay in their own home simply because we did not know how long we would be away, and I wanted them to feel some sense of security while we were gone. Ruby was so gracious to us; she told us she would stay as long as was needed, remarking that we were like family to her, and she wanted to do whatever she could to help. Nicole had recently turned eighteen and was capable of taking care of her brother, but we felt that with the uncertainty of the operation and its outcome, it would not be wise to leave them alone. With that, we packed an overnight bag and left for New York the night before the surgery. I remember how difficult it was to know what to pack for him, not knowing how long he would be there or even what he would be able to wear while he was in recovery. It's not like we were going on vacation—at least cruise ships always give you an idea of what to bring to make your time on the boat comfortable. So, what do you bring to be comfortable in a recovery room? Was comfort even possible anymore? It was all I could do to keep my mind from contemplating all the possible outcomes of our hospital stay, good and bad. Doing the best I could with limited information, I decided on a pair of pajamas, a robe, sweats, and some socks.

"Good enough...I guess..."

We said good-bye to the children, asked the church to pray, and made our way to New York. We stayed in Yonkers overnight so we could avoid the traffic in the morning as we were told to be at the hospital two hours before the surgery, which was scheduled for 10:00 a.m. Ros' direct supervisor had made plans to meet us in New York for moral support, and Ros' older sister had come back down from Canada... some childhood friends of his had also stopped by the hotel to let us know they were thinking of us and praying for us. When you are going through a life-changing event such as this, it is always good to know there are people who are thinking about you and praying for you because no matter what the outcome would be, our lives would be forever changed. His childhood friend told him she felt he would be okay because a friend of hers had just come through the same operation and is doing fine. There was a faint smile on Ros' face as if to say, *Well, maybe there is hope for me,* but as we came through the front door of the hotel on our way to the car, she pulled me aside and told me that she just wanted to cheer him up—she really did not know anyone who survived such an operation. The last thing that I wanted to feel that morning was anger, so I simply stared at her and thought to myself, *silence is golden.*

As we made our way into Manhattan en route to the hospital, the phone rang—it was Nicole calling to tell us she had just received her acceptance letter to Lehigh University. What should have been an accomplished occasion was overshadowed by the roller coaster of events that this cancer set off in our lives. I drove as cautiously as I could into the city, hoping and praying that this would be the last drive we would make under these circumstances. Traffic was at its peak as cab drivers blared their horns, maneuvering their way in and out of traffic, while pedestrians guarded their steps crossing at busy intersections. *I could never live in this city*, I whispered to myself, forgetting that back in the eighties I actually did live there for a short time.

But driving around the city now, that all seemed like a lifetime ago. I circled Sloan Kettering several times before finding a place to park, knowing I would have to come out several times during the day to put coins in the meter, but that was the least of my worries. The walk into Sloan was quite solemn—every step became more difficult than the one before. It felt as if I had iron for feet. I thought, *if I feel this way, what must Ros be feeling? He's the one actually going through the surgery...* I couldn't imagine the turmoil he was feeling inside and to be honest, I was afraid to ask.

We made our way into the hospital and were immediately escorted into the surgical prep area. It's hard to describe how terrifying that area was for me: I had never in my life seen anyone prepped for major surgery before. When I was a teenager, I had several cysts removed from my breast, but I was fully awake. The doctor froze my breast and removed the cysts that same day. But this...this was like something out of a science fiction movie. I had a sudden urge to turn and run, but I doubt I could have found my way out through the maze of corridors. As they began to prep Ros for surgery, the doctors placed what seemed like sand bags or some kind of weight on his ankles, his arms, and his chest. Someone put a plastic cap of sorts on his head while his hands were in restraints... thoughts of a psychiatric ward ran through my mind... *maybe this is how they restrain someone who is being uncooperative.* I was glad that I had begun memorizing scriptures because I found myself repeating them as I stood and watched a host of doctors and nurses prepare my husband for what would be the longest six to seven hours of our lives. The first scripture that came to my mind was, "The Lord has not given me the spirit of fear, but of power and of love and of a sound mind" (ref). And of course, the bishop had given us the scripture about God's perfect love casting out all fear... truly the word of God sustained me that day. As the preparation for the surgery ended, Ros and I held hands, prayed, and asked for God's perfect will to be done. I discovered one thing during that prayer: when we ask for God's perfect will, our hearts are not always in agreement with what our mouths are saying. I found myself saying *your perfect will*, but what happens when his perfect will does not agree with what I want?

I was escorted from the prep room to the waiting area by one of the nurses. Since we were told this surgery would take six to seven hours, I was totally prepared to be there all day. I had several books to read, and Rick had gotten me coffee. We joked about how Ros had tried desperately to get me to cut down on my caffeine intake and how I thought I was making progress when I went from five cups a day to four. I had taken Ros' cell phone so I could call the children the moment it was over to let them know their father was going to be all right. Sitting in a quiet corner of the waiting room, Rick and I spoke about how difficult the recuperation process was going to be; but I told him I was up to it, and he offered his help—anything I needed, he would be willing to help with, he said. I started to say something to my sister-in-law who was sitting across from me when a nurse entered the waiting room.

"Mrs. Robertson, your husband is out of surgery, and the doctor would like to see you in his office..."

Out of surgery... out of surgery...

I found myself repeating her words, but they didn't make sense...that couldn't be possible—he told me six to eight hours... it hasn't even been an hour and a half since I left him... I know because I had only gone once to put coins in the meter...

The room and everything in it began to spin, and I found myself on the dirty floor of Sloan Kettering waiting room. A spirit of hopelessness gripped my heart so that no earthly language came from my lips—only the language that Heaven could understand, ft was no longer an earthly situation—Heaven had stepped in and removed this from my hands. That perfect will I had prayed for in the prep room was not in accordance with what I believed his perfect will should be. Now we *did* have a problem. I had no idea who, but someone helped me up off the floor, and Rick, my sister-in-law, and I walked to the doctor's office... I had no legs to manage standing on my own—mine were legs without bones, limbs so shattered by grief they could barely bear any weight. We walked to the doctor's office, and someone sat me down in a chair. I heard the doctor speaking... even though he was right in front of me, his voice sounded so far away...

"I am sorry, Mrs. Robertson, when we opened your husband's stomach, we simply had to close it back. He has legions of tumors, and the smallest one is bigger than a grapefruit. If we attempted to operate, he would have died right there on the table. I am so sorry to tell you your husband has six months to live..."

I sat there for what seemed like an enormous amount of time. I had long suspected that this was bad, but no one up to this point had put a time frame on his life. *Six months... six months....* how many times in that office I repeated those words, I am not sure, but six months in my mind took on various rhythmic patterns... and now, I had the dubious task of going to the recovery room to tell him he had six months to live... How do you tell the love of your life, the father of your children... your soul mate that he has six months to live? I walked into that recovery room with all the strength I could muster, putting on my everything-is-okay face once again... I thought I had gotten rid of that face, but a sense of relief quickly came over me when I walked into the recovery room, and he was still under the anesthetic, giving me just a little more time to perfect my fake smile. I had become a master at this by now; after all, practice does make perfect.

I sat in that chair for the next hour and watched as his stomach rose and fell, realizing that, in six months, there would be no more rise and fall to his breathing. Overcome by this thought, the tears began to flow, and I had to find a place to hide... the only place I could find was a rest room at the end of the corridor. I ran in, locked the door behind me, and cried uncontrollably. Suddenly, I was instantaneously transported to another hospital a few years back in a rest room just like this one, where I put my fist through the bathroom mirror after witnessing the death of my favorite aunt Edith. Only this time, there was no strength in me to break anything... I was broken, and all that I held dear was now fading out of sight, as if it never existed... it's unclear how long I spent in that bathroom; I know several people tried to come in only to find the door locked... something tells me I was in there for quite some time, and that maybe I should get back to the room in case someone was looking for me. When I did finally make it back to that recovery room, Ros was awake, surrounded by everyone who seemed to be making small talk, avoiding what they knew to be the inevitable question...

"Did they get it all?" he asked me point-blank.

"No," I said, "but they are going to try something else."

He saw right through my lie.

"How long do I have?"

Though *six months* still rhythmically flowed through my mind, the words could not make their way to my mouth.

We left Sloan Kettering that same day. Dr. Fong said it was okay for him to travel since the surgery did not take place. His nurse wheeled him to the front entrance while I went across the street to bring the car closer. As the nurse helped him into the car, I saw the same look of despair on Ros' face that I saw weeks before as we left the parking lot of Yale. Except in this case, a time frame was placed on his life—*six months!* As we pulled out of the city, I put on a CD to fill the anticipated gulf of silence. We drove back to Connecticut without saying a word—what was there to say? I avoided the question during the drive home, but I knew he would ask again. I did everything to delay having to breathe life into that answer. What could I say to six months when we had planned a lifetime together? Six months made no sense to me, and there was nothing I could say to him—words were futile.

The weeks following the death sentence from Sloan Kettering were difficult to say the least. Ros sank into a deep depression. He made me tell him how long the doctor said he had to live, stating that he had every right to know. He was right—who was I to keep that information from him? But once the words came out, I wanted to say that it was all some great big hoax, but what a cruel joke, one that couldn't be taken back, out there for the entire world to hear.

*A*fter some time, the medication Ros took could no longer control the enormity of the pain he experienced. The pain got so intense and so unbearable that we ended up in the hospital three times in less than a month and a half. That third trip to the emergency room is so clear in my mind because it was the first day of my vacation. I requested some time off from work because it was becoming increasingly difficult to work and take care of Ros at the same time. Dispensing medications and generally caring for someone with a terminal illness became a daily routine for me. I started work at 8:00am; at noon, I'd rush home to make him lunch and be back at work in half an hour. I was thankful I worked only five minutes from my house. Because my days became so frantic, rushing from one destination to another, I ran right past my bishop's wife one day, almost knocking her out of the way before I realized it was her. I quickly apologized and told her I had to go home and make lunch and be back in half an hour so I could not stop to talk. She told me she understood and commented that the church was praying for us.

I was physically and emotionally exhausted from the constant travelling back and forth from hospitals and from the stress of just going through Ros' illness, so I decided to take a week off from work just to get my bearings and try to put some things into perspective. On that first day of my vacation, which happened to be a Saturday morning, I was really looking forward to taking things down a notch, ft was late that Friday night when I finally drifted off to sleep because in spite of all the medication I had given him, it was nearly impossible to manage his pain. The agony seemed to have risen to a new dimension; and no matter what we did, there seemed to be no comfort for him. As I look back, it was one of the few times my husband had asked me to stay with him in the room as if he had some notion that something was going to happen.

I remember slipping out in the wee hours of the morning when I thought he found some small measure of relief. That Saturday morning, though, I awoke to a sound I had never heard before. For a few moments, I just laid there, trying to figure out where I was and what exactly I was hearing... it suddenly dawned on me that the sound was coming from the opposite room—it was Ros, and he was in great distress. I sprang out of the bed like a gymnast only to find him on the floor in the most extreme pain I had ever seen him in. My attempt to lift him from off the floor was futile— it seemed that overnight, his weight had doubled, making it impossible for one person to get him up. Once again, the ambulance was at our door, rushing him for another trip to the hospital. It had become increasingly clear that this illness was getting more violent as the days dragged on. It seemed that our time was spent mostly in ambulances and hospital rooms. I felt like an ambulance chaser, following behind those speeding sirens in my own car so that we would have transportation back home when Ros was released. We were constantly fighting an uphill battle, and it was hard to get a grip. I continued to believe there was a miracle in store for us, but it was hard to look beyond where we were: to think that Ros would not make it would be to give in to this monster that had invaded our lives.

It was not just the disease itself that we had problems coming to terms with—it was the way this illness had consumed all of us who were a part of Ros' life. He and I no longer shared the intimacy as man and wife: now my role was changed to caregiver, dispensing medication, and giving baths and haircuts, making sure Ros was as comfortable as possible. This disease consumed the children's lives as well: Nicole turned eighteen, and Jordan turned eight in the midst of all this, but the focus could not be on them because this illness required all my attention and energy. My neighbor who ran a bowling league put together a birthday party for Jordan since he bowled for her team. Unfortunately, nothing was done for Nicole that year in terms of a celebration because I was consumed with caring for Ros. She did travel to San Francisco with her school choir around her birthday, so that lessened my guilt; up until that point, she had always had a birthday party... it was something I enjoyed doing for the children over the years. It was their special day, and it needed to be recognized.

The day after Ros came back from that last emergency visit, I was in prayer and wanted to know why there did not seem to be an answer for us. So many people were praying for him, and so many had fasted including me. Ros had even gone to a well-known faith healer, but his situation grew worse, not better. I wanted to know from the Almighty, the Jehovah Rapha—what was the problem? Here, we had prayed with all the sincerity that we could... we had asked in faith, believing that the Lord would hear and answer our prayers—who, faced with a disease as devastating as cancer, would ask for healing so casually? Then what was the problem? I felt the Spirit of the Lord pose a question in my spirit: *HOW WOULD YOU WORSHIP ME IF HE WAS HEALED?* I didn't know how to answer that question, but that night, I got out of bed and began to sing and dance in the spirit as I had never done before because I wanted the Lord to know I was willing to do whatever it would take to prepare for that miraculous healing I knew would take place. I sang and danced that night until I collapsed from sheer exhaustion with not an ounce of energy to spare.

At this point in our fight against cancer—and I say *our* fight because it was not just Ros that had cancer—I felt like we were all suffering from it in one way or another. We may not have had the physical scars of the illness, but emotionally, we were all plagued. I remember how upset Ros got when his illness was mentioned in the church bulletin so that prayer would be offered up on his behalf. He was upset, saying that now, our names would no longer be mentioned without the stigma of cancer attached. In his mind, everyone was saying, "There goes Brother Robertson—he has cancer;" "You know, there goes Sister Robertson—her husband has cancer," or "There goes Nicole and Jordan Robertson; their father has cancer," as if it were some leprous plague that we somehow called on ourselves or warranted sympathy from all who heard our plight. Never again would our names seemingly be mentioned without the attachment of cancer. Although I told him I did not care what people thought, I really wanted to scream it to the world that we did nothing to deserve this. We were unjustly punished for some terrible crime we didn't commit, making us victims unwilling to participate in the drama that unfolded around us.

By now, the main hallway of our house was covered with scriptures I had posted on the wall; whenever I passed by, I would linger long enough to read some of them. Without those scriptures, I don't believe I would have made it through those difficult days. One particular morning after Ros returned from the hospital, my eyes caught Isaiah 61:3, "To appoint unto them that mourn in Zion, to give unto them beauty for ashes, the oil of joy for mourning, the garment of praise for the spirit of heaviness; that they might be called trees of righteousness, the planting of the Lord, that He might be glorified." I began to ask myself the question: *Is God being glorified in all of this?* Would "trees of righteousness" be an appropriate descriptor for us? Walking to the living room, I wanted to hear something that would calm my troubled spirit. I found a tape I had recently purchased. As the soothing melodies streamed from the speakers, I heard a rich soprano voice sing: "He gives beauty for ashes, strength for fear; gladness for mourning, peace for despair..." As those words rang in my ear, I wept uncontrollably. I don't recall how long I was there weeping, but somewhere in the midst of my tears, I heard a voice.

"Honey, it's not that bad; it will be alright."

Ros' tone was somber, so I knew it was that bad. In all of this, I had missed the purpose altogether. This illness was not meant to break us but to build us into those trees of righteousness so that God would be glorified in everything, even in the midst of this most trying time.

I was weeping because the revelation became clear: in that moment, I understood that God was in control of this situation, and my hands had to be open to let him do whatever He saw fit. This was a test of our faith. In this darkest moment of our lives, would we continue to hold on to all that we said we believed, or would we cave into the pressure, reducing our relationship with Christ to nothing more than some feel-good rituals that somehow justified our existence? The question I needed to ask myself was not *"How would I worship if he was healed?"* but *"Would I worship Jesus Christ, even if the physical healing did not come?"*

And all that became clear in that one line of that song... **He** *gives beauty for ashes... strength for fear... gladness for mourning... peace for despair...* it was a great exchange, but I was too busy holding on to despair and fear to receive His peace, His love, and His grace which are more than sufficient, even for cancer and everything that came with it.

That in and of itself was a difficult idea to come to grips with. Now that understanding had somewhat enlightened my mind, my prayer and my attitude had to change. Instead of asking, *"Lord, please heal,"* I had to be ready to say, *"Lord, your will be done."* How uncomfortable it is to let go when you have held on to something—anything—for so long. So, after this revelation, I began a forty-day fast. I didn't know what to do next, so the next best thing I thought would be to fast and pray. It's not that we hadn't been praying before, but the Bible tells us that some things don't come out except through fasting and praying. When I had this bright idea, I perhaps should have consulted a physician or at least have gotten some spiritual guidance before venturing on a road I had never been down before. Then again, I had always been of the mind-set that if you are going to do something, you jump in with both feet and suffer the consequences later. Probably not the best motto to go by in this case: at the end of two weeks, I was getting dressed for work one morning and did not recognize the person who stared back at me in the mirror. I had lost so much weight that I was looking at a stranger. As I got out of my car that morning in the parking lot at work, I stepped right out of my skirt and would have kept on walking if my skirt hadn't tried to trip me! Luckily, it was early in the morning, and the parking lot was empty. I pulled my skirt up and went tentatively on my way, trying to maintain some form of dignity.

Only four months since the initial diagnosis, and the illness was rapidly taking its toll. Ros had lost so much weight, and his stomach was protruding worse than ever before. I was sinking into a deep depression that I did not think I would recover from. Everything around me seemed so hopeless. That summer, we bought Jordan a basketball hoop, and I watched Ros struggle to put it together. What would have taken him an hour when he was healthy took him several days. I watched him struggle with every ounce of strength he had, as if he knew this would be the last thing he would do for his son. Since that devastating trip to Sloan, we lived every day in uncertainty, not sure what our next step would or should be. Every ounce of hope we had was taken from us—where could we go from there? How could we make any real plans when he had six months to live? We did plan a trip to celebrate our anniversary which we missed in June because of all the hospital visits. Ros wanted to take a trip back to Jamaica, the land of our birth. I was not able to leave until the end of July because of all the time I had missed going back and forth from the hospital. Ros decided he would go with Jordan, and I would join them at the end of July. Despite the invasion of cancer in our lives, we would try to have some type of anniversary celebration, although to be honest, my heart was so heavy that I didn't see how it was possible to celebrate anything in the midst of all that despair. But for Ros' sake, I was willing to do my best. I donned my everything-is-okay face as my husband and son boarded the plane and started their vacation. For the first time in four months, I was able to sleep through the night. What a sense of relief and guilt I felt all at the same time: relief because I could actually sleep without having to worry about administering medication for his pain, but guilt realizing that this illness was nothing of his doing. Ros' pain had just become so unbearable for him that it was impossible for anyone to sleep through any night with the constant flurry of activity that came with dispensing pain medications several times to try to subdue the deep moans he stifled when the pain got to be too much for his body to handle.

I left for Jamaica one month later at the end of July to join Ros and my son in hopes of what would be some form of a vacation, feeling rather guilty that Nicole could not make the trip since she had just gotten a summer job at one of the branches of the bank I worked for. She started taking on some of her mother's attributes with her own everything-is-okay face, knowing there was nothing more she would rather do than be with her family, especially considering the uncertainty of the days ahead. Even though vacation was the furthest thing from my mind, nothing could have prepared me for the sight I would see awaiting me at the airport. The beautiful man I had married nine years earlier was not the same man standing before me: if Jordan hadn't been with him, I would not have recognized my husband. His face was gaunt, and his stomach protruded from beneath the shirt he was wearing like the womb of a woman ready to give birth. It was hard to believe that in one month, this disease had terrorized his body so much to make him look almost unrecognizable. No matter how hard I tried, it was difficult to focus on anything other than the way he looked standing there. I stared at him longer than I intended to; the very sight of him caught me off guard, and he must have seen the shocked look on my face because the kiss he gave me when we finally drew near was incredibly tense, as if he was afraid to approach me. My attention immediately turned to Jordan so that there would be something else to focus on; but as we made our way to the car, I stole momentary glances at this man I had promised to spend the rest of my life with, for better and for worse, in sickness and in health... My mind could not believe what my eyes were seeing; and my heart, not sure what to feel, was a helpless victim of the war between the two.

Ros had made plans for us to spend our anniversary away from the rest of the family we were staying with, reserving a room at one of the finer hotels on the island. As I walked into that hotel room and saw the preparations he had made in anticipation of our anniversary celebration, all I wanted to do was run. For a moment, all I could think about was finding some way to escape that night, and yet the tenderness of his heart and the overwhelming love a husband had for his wife compelled me to stay. Even with this demon called cancer trying to stand between us, we had made a covenant—a sacred vow—and I would be his and he mine until the covenant was broken, so help us God.

The day following that night, I had a new resolve: although I did not folly understand God's purpose for all that we were experiencing, I knew there had to be a purpose, so I made up my mind to think like Job: though He slay me, yet will I trust Him. That didn't stop the questioning, though— what *was* the purpose for all of this?

While we were in Jamaica, we drove from one end of the island to the other to visit my grandmother who was living through the last stages of Alzheimer's disease. The experience was surreal—we were strangers to her, and as I stared at the face of this woman who had raised me as her own child, I saw in her eyes a distant look that I later came to understand was indicative of the beginning of her transcendental journey from this life to the next. When we went back home, I immediately called my mother in Florida and my aunt in Toronto to tell them they should make plans to go see their mother because when I looked into those eyes, something told me it would not be long for her.

By the time we left Jamaica and flew back to Connecticut, Ros' weight had plummeted to an all-time low. He barely made a hundred pounds. Back in our "normal" routine (whatever that meant), I started him on a regiment of fresh juices, trying anything to help him maintain or even gain some weight. Wherever we went, we carried a thermos of soup or juice as a means of encouraging his appetite. On one particular visit to the doctor, the scale showed that he had gained a pound—I got so excited over that one pound, looking for any glimmer of hope that we could hang on to... turns out that the weight gain came from the tumors that were growing rapidly—that in itself was another devastating blow. Every visit to the doctors after that seemed more and more hopeless. I wondered to myself why we kept going when it was clear that medicine had nothing else to offer us. We were just going through the motions with doctors who all seemed so compassionless as if they were immune to the pains of impending death. Maybe seeing people clinging so desperately to life had become a normal phenomenon for them, but this was not normal for us—this was my husband's life... our *lives*... and it was quickly spiraling out of our grasp. With the exception of Dr. Alfano who made the initial diagnosis, Ros was just another face in the crowded picture of terminal illness. To have a physician—even just one—empathize with us as we faced the premature end of life would probably have been too much to ask. One doctor, in the middle of his examination, just shook his head as he put the stethoscope to Ros' chest as if to say, *there is no hope for you.* I remember the tears rolling down my husband's face as that doctor finished his examination. I'm almost certain that was the moment it finally dawned on Ros that this was the end of the road for him. Whatever hope may have lingered up to that point gave way to the bitter acceptance that our lives and the lives of our children would never be the same.

Nicole was getting ready to leave for college in late August of 1999. We rented a van to pack up and move her things to Lehigh University in Bethlehem, Pennsylvania. That should have been one of the happiest times of our lives. After all, it's not every day your child goes off to college and starts another chapter of her life... and yet we were so preoccupied with the side effects of illness that what should have been a celebratory moment went virtually unnoticed. My husband packed her things in that van with such care—he placed every item so precisely and particularly, knowing he would probably never have the opportunity to do much more for her again. He stopped to take short breaths and rest after he put each item in its place. It was so tempting to go and help, but I thought that would just validate the fact that he was no longer capable of doing even the simplest of things he once took for granted. I watched from the bedroom window as he folded the backseat of that van so every item she wanted to take with her would fit, resting after even the slightest movement so that he would have energy for the next one. It's amazing the feeling of helplessness you experience when you are in a situation that is completely out of your control. Every action, each minute, decisions became a cause for scrutiny: is there something I could have done to prevent this? Is there something that I'm *not* doing now to help the situation?

My mind ran every mile of what should have been a three-hour trip from Waterbury to Bethlehem. I say *should* have been because, now, frequent stops were a norm for even the shortest of road trips. We tried our best to make Ros feel comfortable during the ride, but it was so difficult since nothing we did seemed to make a difference. He was so weak and weary by the time we got to our destination that it took several doses of all kinds of pain killers at varied intervals during the trip just to take the edge off.

Ros was too weak to participate in any of the evening activities waiting for us when we arrived on the sprawling green campus. After the welcoming committee and ROTC soldiers quickly unloaded our rental van and packed Nicole's things into her dorm room, the rest of us retired to the hotel while she explored her new home. Ros encouraged me to go and spend time with our daughter. I felt guilty about leaving him, but it was nice to have a diversion from his pain and my torturing thoughts, even if only for a short while. He and Jordan stayed in the hotel room while my friend Jeanetta, who had accompanied us on the trip, and I met up with Nicole back on campus. She was already finding her way around and brought us to an enjoyable night at the opera. That was the night my friend and I discovered Nutrageous ice cream by Ben and Jerry's. Although Ros could not eat it, Jordan had a great big smile on his face as he devoured the contents of the tub we brought back to the room. It was little moments like these that helped us forget about the despair in our hearts, even if only for a moment.

The next day, we said our good-byes to Nicole and started on our way back to Connecticut. I drove all the way home because Ros was in too much discomfort to concentrate on driving. There were such long periods of silence during that ride. Everyone seemed much too afraid to be the first to speak, so we all kept silent, which only magnified Ros' deep moans whenever a surge of pain came on. All eyes would turn to see what we could do for him, knowing that there wasn't much we could do at this point but give him drugs and pray that it would bring some relief even for a short while.

Back at home, we tried to fall into a normal routine, but with Nikki off in another state at school and Ros' illness ruling our every move, I couldn't tell you what normal was. I would burst into tears every time I walked by her room and saw her stripped bed and empty shelves. I knew the routine we had gotten accustomed to would never be the same—who knows where she would go after graduating from college? The dull ache in my heart steadily grew as I pondered what the future held for all of us.

With each passing day, it seemed like more of a struggle for Ros to get out of bed. While my aunt was visiting us from Florida, she suggested moving Ros into Nikki's room, seeing how no one was using it anyway. Truth be told, I was hesitant to make the move: I certainly didn't want him feeling more isolated than he did already, now that he was pretty much limited to staying in the house. Emotions fought violently against reason, but in the end, we all knew it was the best option for him. That move accomplished two things: 1) I no longer fell apart whenever I passed by the room because, now, it was occupied again; and 2) it was so much easier for Ros to get on and off the soft padding on the solid mattress as opposed to trying to maneuver his way in and out of the waterbed we had shared since our youngest was born.

The mattress seemed to provide some relief, but any relief was short-lived as the bombastic tumors waged a never-ending war against every pain receptor in his body. Still, not once did I hear a complaint from Ros as to why this was happening to him. When I would break down in tears, thinking about how hopeless and destitute our situation seemed, I'd hear him reassuringly say, "Honey, it's not that bad; we will get through this," but it *was* that bad, and there *were* days when I was convinced we would never get through this low point in our lives. That smile that once lit up a room was now distorted by constant pain and anguish. That smile that once spoke of love and anticipation for the future now turned into a twisted symbol of agony.

The weeks following Nikki's departure for school grew more and more difficult. There was not a moment in the day when Ros did not seem to be in pain. He consumed pills like candy that gave only momentary relief from the anguishing attacks. Just when I thought things couldn't get any worse, the bottom would fall out, and we'd find ourselves at a whole new level of "worse" that neither of us thought was possible. One Saturday morning, I woke up to a loud thump in the house. It hadn't been long since I last drifted to sleep—4:30 in the morning, to be precise. The bright neon alarm clock portrayed the time as I laid down next to Ros on the bed, singing and praying since that seemed to be the only medication that worked to soothe his pain. When he finally drifted off to sleep, I quietly slipped out of the room to try and get some rest myself before a new day began. An hour later, the thump jolted me out of my sleep. It took me a minute or two to realize what was happening, but after I made the adjustment to conscious mode and sprang to Ros' room, I found him down on the ground, wedged between the bed and the side table. He had tried to make his way to the bathroom, only to find out that his legs could not sustain his body weight. I called for Jordan to lend me a hand, and we tried unsuccessfully to lift him off the ground—it was an impossible task that brought the ambulance back to our doorstep. I could only imagine what our neighbors thought was happening every time those flashing lights lit down our street and stopped right in from of our door. I caught a few curious eyes peering through the windows when they thought no one was looking... if I were in their shoes, I would probably have done the same thing.

As the EMTs rushed through the door, I heard Ros say something, and the paramedics stopped in their tracks. There was a sense of urgency in his voice; and as I drew closer, I heard him say, "I want to see my son before I leave." He was adamant about not leaving until he spoke with Jordan. I called Jordan, who timidly came out from his room, still dressed in his blue dinosaur pajamas. He walked apprehensively to his father's side, not knowing what to expect. Ros whispered something to him in a quiet tone; then, I saw him slip something into Jordan's hand. I knew there wasn't anything in Ros' hands for him to give to his son. When Jordan and I had attempted to get him off the floor, his hands were empty. Satisfied, Ros gave the signal for the paramedics to move out. The EMTs continued out the door as I stood there, wondering what had just transpired between father and son.

When we came home from the hospital the next day, I checked the mailbox and found an interesting piece of mail—it was a letter confirming that I had been granted American citizenship and inviting me to participate in the swearing-in ceremony. I had applied for citizenship almost a year before, but with Ros' illness consuming our lives, the anticipated citizenship had been the furthest thing from my mind. This should have been a very exciting time for me, but I just sat at the kitchen table, staring blankly at the letter, something I had once looked forward to now seemed so unimportant... so trivial, knowing that, in a few months, my husband wouldn't be here to share it with me. Tears welled up in my eyes as I stared numbly at the letter. Hearing the shuffle of Ros' slippers in the hallway, I quickly wiped my face and found something to occupy myself with in the kitchen.

He made the short trek from his room to the kitchen and gingerly sat down at the table. Seeing the invitation I had left in my haste, Ros looked up at me and smiled.

"Welcome to America."

"Ha, ha, ha," I retorted.

"We should call Bishop and Sister Ruby to go with us."

"I'm not going," I replied.

"Why not?"

I gave him a look as if to say, *you know why I'm not going.*

"Honey, I may be sick; but I'm not dead yet. You're not going to miss an important event like this on account of me. Now what time should I tell Bishop and Sister Ruby to meet us?"

For someone who was sick, he sure was pretty convincing. In my mind, it made no sense to drive forty-five minutes to the state capitol for a silly ceremony that would last half that time, but Ros was so adamant about not letting this disease rob us of everything. As ill as he was, he still had that stubborn spirit. Not wanting to fight with him, I begrudgingly gave in to his persistence.

The day of the ceremony, we got in the car to make our way to the capitol. I still did not think it was a good idea for Ros to go with me to the swearing-in, but he so wanted to be with me during that supposedly momentous day. Pain and all, he made the trip and sat through all the speeches and legalities. I remember packing a thermos with soup in it so that when he got hungry, he could have something to eat, no matter where we were. At this point, it had become virtually impossible for him to eat any kind of solid food. The most he could hold down at times was a bit of soup. A metallic gray thermos soon became a constant accessory whenever we went out, which became less and less as the tumors fought back more and more.

The days became long and tedious for Ros. On several "good" days when his pain was less severe, his stubborn spirit drove him to attempt a trip to his workplace. Most days, he only made it to the bottom of the basement stairs by the garage. On the few occasions where he made it beyond the stairs, I felt a cautious sense of optimism. After all, if he could make it to the car and eventually to work, I could begin to convince myself that things were not as bad as they seemed. Inevitably, though, the garage door would open again, and I'd find Ros slumped over the steering wheel, unable to get out of the car because of the enormity of the pain he felt. One particular morning, he had gotten up and got dressed as had been his normal routine. I offered to make him something to eat, but he insisted on just some hot tea. Thermos in hand, he made his way to the garage, and I listened intently for any signs of distress. The garage door opened, and then I heard it close. Then I waited and waited... I waited so long that I must have fallen asleep because the next time I noticed the clock, it was an hour later. Thankful that he seemingly had the energy to make it out of the house, I started my daily chores, feeling a little lighter, knowing this would be a "good" day. But good quickly turned sour as I went downstairs to put a load of laundry in the machine. As I opened the garage door, there was Ros, slumped over the steering wheel in great pain. He never made it beyond the garage.

Every day, it seemed that something would happen to confirm that our situation was quickly turning from bad to worse. When I looked at him, I felt as if I were watching his body deteriorate before my eyes. Completely helpless, there was nothing I could do about it. As human beings, we judge a situation by what we see: if something looks good, we assume it to be good; likewise, if it looks bad, we say it must be bad. All my natural eyes could see was bad at this point; but I forced myself to see that even though everything looked bad right then, he was the same man I married nine years before. Even though his physique had deteriorated, the compassion he had before this invasion was still there: he still loved with a relentless love and still pushed to do whatever he could to take care of his family. The essence of who he was still lived even if his body was just a shell of its former self. At times, I found myself just staring at him, completely lost in thought. One of those journeys took me back to another place and time when I had met this young man at a church play in Montreal. He asked me to marry him, and I said no because I knew he had come out of a tumultuous relationship—that was certainly not something I wanted to be a part of. But he was persistent, asking me three times to be his wife. The third time, the proposal came with a promise: *marry me; I'm going to be rich.* What woman could resist such a statement? Yet I knew in my heart of hearts that it wasn't the promise of riches that made me change my mind. Ros was so much deeper than that, his captivating smile betraying the fact that he really believed what he said. I remember him promising that it would all work out if I just said yes... looking back to that now distorted smile; I'm pretty sure this was not what he had in mind. Even so, looking at him in that state, I wondered if I had seen this coming if I still would have said yes, knowing full well that no amount of pain or anguish could erase the sheer joy we shared as a family. I was lost in that moment of nostalgia when I heard him speak.

"Honey, we need to give them a raise."

The question jolted me back to reality.

"Give who a raise?" I asked.

"The family that is building the fence for us."

For a minute, I thought I was lost in some kind of alternate reality. Timidly, I asked the next logical question.

"Uh, which family that is building the fence for us?"

"The ones down there. See how diligent they are working to get the fence done in time for us? Every one of them is working as hard as they can. They deserve a raise."

His tone was so serious that I didn't know if I should laugh, check his forehead, or go outside myself to see what was going on. But staring out the window, he began to describe with such vivid detail the members of this "family." I knew he was seeing *something*, but there was no natural family outside our house—at least, not that I could see. But the fervor with which he spoke made me wonder if he was seeing with something other than his physical eyes. Family and friends everywhere were praying for us, and I found out later that the focus of their prayers was that the Lord would send his angels to build a hedge around us. Could this be the family he was seeing? I was still contemplating Ros' vision a few days later when he called me into his room.

"Honey?"

"Yeah," I answered, dish towel in hand.

"Can you do me a favor?" he asked.

"Sure, what do you need?"

"Would you mind helping the elderly lady sitting in this chair here cross the street? It's so busy, and I don't want her to get hurt."

There was a chair in the room, but I certainly didn't see any elderly lady sitting in it. I almost wished that I could because Ros kept insisting that she needed someone to help her get across the street safely. I kept looking at him and looking at the chair then said what any sane person would have done in my position...

"Okay...."

Seeming quite content, Ros smiled and closed his eyes as he turned on his side for his afternoon nap. I was so glad his eyes were closed so that he couldn't see the bewildered look on my face. How are you supposed to escort an invisible elderly lady across the street?

By the latter part of October 1999, the tumors had grown so big that they were clearly visible no matter what Ros wore, ft was abundantly clear at this point that help was desperately needed to care for him. Even though he was still somewhat mobile, he had become so weak that he didn't even attempt to leave the house any more. Putting him in hospice care was never an option; when he first became ill and we realized how serious his condition was, he had asked me not put him in a hospital if ever he was incapable of taking care of himself. I gave him my word, but it became more and more challenging to work and give him the best care. When I spoke to his physician and asked for a referral to get some assistance, especially during the daytime when I had to leave for work, I was told that no one would come unless Ros was completely bedridden. Once again, I turned to the only place I had found any real help since this ordeal began. Our church family, the body of Christ, started taking turns staying with Ros while I was at work. One person would come in the morning before I left; then in the afternoon, someone else would come to relieve the morning shift, just like the changing of the guards. They came faithfully, a fact I was eternally thankful for. Without their support, I doubt I could have survived the ordeal. One particular friend, when he realized how desperate our situation was, would come to the house after he got off of work—he worked second shift, so that meant eleven o'clock at night. Instead of going home to his family, he drove thirty minutes out of his way to my house and sat in his truck and prayed for my family that the Lord would see us through those difficult days. I felt so bad for him that I would go out to offer him a drink of coffee or a soda or something, but each time, he would just tell me that I didn't have to bring him anything; he just wanted us to know that he was there praying for our family. Words can't even begin to describe how acts of kindness and thoughtfulness such as this one lifted my spirits. Every time I thought I would just let go and fall to pieces, I'd think of that saint of God and so many more like him who were praying for us. Their prayers gave me the strength to hang on for another day.

As the fall drew on and leaves began to change, there was something different in the air. There was no anticipation for the Thanksgiving holiday except for the fact that it meant my mother and aunt would fly up from Florida to give us a hand, and Nicole would come home from school for her first break. For a little while, just having the family together took our minds off the situation at hand. It was only when I started to smile a bit more and heard Ros and Jordan laugh when I realized those elements had been absent in our home. But as soon as we began to relax in our environment again, something happened to remind us that we were living on borrowed time. One evening after dinner, we sat in our living room watching "Jeopardy!" and having normal conversation when suddenly, Ros, whose head had been comfortably resting in my lap, jumped up and declared to everyone in the room that he was dying. Looks of fear and confusion flashed on everyone's face, wondering what to do or say next. Thank goodness, my mother, a licensed practical nurse, had the good sense to take his pulse. Finding it completely normal, she calmed him down and tried to convince him that he still had some life left in him. No matter what she said, though, Ros was convinced that he wouldn't make it through the night. Not knowing what else to do, I called the number of a visiting nurse referred to us by a family friend who would come by on occasion to see if there was anything he could do. He was at the house within the hour, taking Ros' pulse and blood pressure, which were both perfectly normal. With no explanation for the outburst, the nurse speculated that perhaps, while he slept, he dreamt about his own death and was convinced it was taking place at that very moment. Whatever the reason for the outburst, it put a damper on the rest of the all-too-short celebration. The Thanksgiving holiday came and went all too quickly: my mother and aunt went back to Florida, Nicole left again for school, and once again, I was faced with the impending death of a husband and a young child to console when all was said and done.

After Ros' Thanksgiving outburst, we made several visits to his personal physician. Of course, it all seemed so pointless since there was nothing left for the doctor to do but to increase his pain medication. One morning as I helped him get washed up and dressed for the day, Ros insisted I give him a haircut. As far as I could see, his hair did not need cutting since it hadn't grown nearly as fast as it did before he got sick. Nevertheless, he insisted, and so I gave him a haircut. When I was finished, he took the small mirror, and gave himself a look over.

"That will do," he stated.

It's very difficult to tell what someone in that kind of condition is thinking or to imagine the reason behind some of their actions. To be perfectly honest, most of the time I was afraid to ask, fearful of the answer I might hear. Then again, I'm not sure which was worse—hearing the real reason behind a seemingly random haircut or seeing the possible scenarios play out in my overactive mind. Drawing your own conclusions can be just as bad if not worse than the truth, and every solution I came up with resulted in a finality I was not ready to face.

By the time the beginning of December rolled around, the doctor finally understood how difficult dealing with this illness was becoming for us when Ros had to be wheeled to his office. He was unable to walk without help, and so the doctor insisted we get some help from hospice. When the word "hospice" traveled from his lips to my ears, whatever glimmer of hope or optimism that once lived deep down inside of me, in a place I could not see, died right there in his office. *Hospice* is nothing more than a fancy word for "point of no return." There is nothing after hospice except death, and we all knew it. On the way home, Ros reiterated he did not want to be placed in a hospital. I had already given him my word, and I wasn't about to turn back now. If the doctor insisted on giving hospice care, hospice care would have to come to us—and that's exactly what happened. Monday morning, bright and early before I left for work, there was a ring of the doorbell. When I opened the door, I saw a petite brunette in front of me with the brightest smile.

"Hi! I'm Annie, the hospice care nurse. Dr. Stephens sent me here to give you a hand with your husband."

Shaking her hand, I welcomed her into the house and brought her to Ros' room to make the introduction. He never looked at her even once, but his gaze was steadfast in my direction as if to say, *so it's come to this?* I gave Annie a quick tour of the house and left for work that morning with the heaviest heart since the whole ordeal had started, even more so than when we received the initial diagnosis. I felt as if I had let him down on every level. I came home at noon to make him lunch as usual, but he refused to eat. Later that week, his older sisters came to spend some time with him. I was glad once again to have other people in the house, but their short visit was more depressing than anything. Their emotional make up was overwhelming for him—instead of offering words of encouragement, all they spoke about were arrangements for a funeral. That got on my last nerve, and so they simply had to go. It's good to be practical—don't get me wrong; but in a desperate situation, one needs to be surrounded by positive people who will believe with you and encourage you no matter what.

If Ros wasn't eating before, the flurry of unexpected visitors certainly didn't do anything to help his appetite. I had him on a regiment of juices I would mix based on nutritional studies and good sense. It became quite a culinary adventure each day to see what juices we could come up with using different vegetables and fruits. Only God himself could have known what an investment it was, making sure he got the nutrients and vitamins he was not getting because of the gag reflex he developed when he saw or even smelled any kind of food. In the course of my research, someone had even suggested that I make him dandelion tea. At that stage, I could easily see myself in desperation, going out to the backyard to harvest dandelions to make tea for my husband. Never underestimate what people will suggest when hopelessness sets in. I knew people were just trying to help because they felt our pain, but what was even more incredible was what I was willing to do to bring an end to this whole nightmare.

By the next week, Ros had such trouble getting in and out of bed that he had to have someone take him to the bathroom that was just across the hall. I often wondered if this illness affected his eyes: there were times when he was looking in my direction, but I affirm he was looking right past me, as if he saw something beyond me. It frightened me so much that I asked Sister Dibble if we could have our monthly ladies' prayer meeting at the house instead of church. It had been months now since Ros had not been able to go to church, and I knew how much he missed assembling with people who believed in the power of Almighty God.

Held on the second Monday of the month, our ladies' prayer was usually well attended; this time around, however, many of the ladies either could not make it or were afraid to come. I suppose at that time, my house could be considered a house of death, and death always makes people fearful or uncomfortable. Regardless, our skeletal crew of three came together to sing, to pray, and to ask for God's guidance in whatever was ahead. We felt the presence of the Lord so evident in that living room... When it was all over and the ladies had gone, Ros called me in the room. He wanted to know how many people were in the house because it sounded like an angelic host. I told him it was just Sister Dibble, Sister Jessica, and me. He said he heard a lot more than just the three of us. He began to describe how he heard voices he did not recognize uniting in harmonious song and ascending to the heavens as steady as the rising sun. I hadn't heard any other voices beside our own, but as I listened to him describe the heavenly host he heard, I wondered if his ears were aligning with the vision his eyes were beginning to see.

I was not going to get a Christmas tree that year. Frankly, there was just too much on my mind and on my plate, things much more important and pressing in my mind to contend with than fussing over a Christmas tree. Even so, a family friend showed up at our door one day with a freshly-cut evergreen. I figured it was an attempt to help us have as normal a Christmas as we possibly could, but even a tray of our favorite Christmas cookies could not get me in the mood to celebrate what had always been our favorite time of the year. Instead, I looked around at all the tokens—the cards, the cookies, the tree—and wondered if these same acts of kindness would have been offered if Ros wasn't sick, and we weren't is such a dismal state. Why is it that, as human beings, we wait until some tragedy or something unfortunate happens before we show random acts of kindness when that should be the norm every day, especially for the people of God? The reason we are called *Christians* is because we are supposed to reflect Christ who did good wherever he went. While I contemplated the lament of humanity, the phone rang—it was Nicole calling from school. She was in the midst of her final exams and was experiencing a terrible pain in her head. I suspect that tremendous pain was due to her desire to come home to her father, feeling out of the loop as to what was really happening. We did what we had done so many times before, we prayed on the phone, and I spoke a few words to encourage her before we hung up. Just then, my friend Deborah came out of Ros' room and into the kitchen where I was still sitting at the table. Deborah was one of those faithful friends who, on many occasions, had come over to sit and read for Ros so I could take a break to run errands, go to church, or just have a moment to myself since someone had to be with him constantly in case he needed to get up or even to dispense medication. On hearing about my conversation with Nicole, she offered to make the drive to Pennsylvania to pick her up right after her last exam so she could be home with her family.

Over the next few days, there was a glimmer of hope in the midst of darkness. I noticed that for a few days, Ros did not seem to need any medication. Bewildered, I would ask if he was in pain, but his answer was always the same: "*no.*" Looking at him, nothing had physically changed over the last few days—his stomach was still protruding, and his handsome face was now gaunt, the light of his eyes having grown so dim that they seemed almost hollow. So, for him not to need any medication was difficult to explain. Not only that, but this same man who needed help to go anywhere and who could not stand the sight of food got up on his own, went to the kitchen, and got some of the Christmas cookies that were arranged on a tray, parked squarely on the countertop. There was no reasonable explanation for his actions... at least, no earthly explanation that made any kind of sense. He seemed to be able to walk with very little help. He then walked to the living room and sat in the sunlight for a change of scenery. Then after falling asleep on the couch, he suddenly broke out in a language that only Heaven could have understood.

When the following week rolled around, it was December 13th-A Monday. It started as any other day of the week with the bishop coming to the house to sit and pray with Ros as he had done so many times before. While I was in the kitchen making coffee for the bishop, Ros walked up behind me, nearly scaring the living daylights out of me.

"I want to go home."

It was a statement I was not expecting. We had just come back from Jamaica following a return trip for my grandmother's funeral the first week of October. Even though it wasn't the best of circumstances, the trip allowed us time to spend with both our families and with Nicole since she was granted leave from school to come for the funeral. As good as the trip was, though, it left Ros exhausted, and I had no intentions of returning any time soon.

"What did you say?" I asked timidly, as any sensible wife would.

"I WANT TO GO HOME."

"... but we just came back from—"

He stopped me in the middle of my sentence.

"I don't mean Jamaica."

... but he had to mean Jamaica: we had spent twenty years living in Canada and another ten years in Connecticut, but he had always considered Jamaica home, so it could be no other place but Jamaica. I called the bishop to the room and told Ros to repeat what he just said to me. In no uncertain terms, Ros repeated his request.

"I WANT TO GO HOME."

Bishop looked intently at Ros. Then after a moment, he gave his assessment.

"Okay."

Now, I consider myself to be a fairly intelligent person—not super smart by any means but reasonably intelligent. But standing there in that kitchen that day, I assumed that I must have missed something; because if I understood correctly, my husband was declaring loud and clear that he was ready to die, and my bishop just agreed that he was indeed ready. Surely, this could not be what they were really saying. They both left me hanging there as if this was the most normal statement in the world. My body stayed put, my feet seemingly stuck in cement, but my mind and emotions ran a mile a minute. In that moment, I went through the gamut of every possible human experience from sheer terror to common sense thinking: I was going to be a forty-two-year-old widow with an eight-year-old son and an eighteen-year-old daughter who had just started college. How in the world did I get to this moment and where do I go from this moment and can somebody PLEASE tell me how to get back to my *real* life—the one where my husband and I raise our children together and watch our babies have babies and retire to somewhere hot where he can take up golf by the beach, and I can pretend I have a green thumb and just mill around the garden all day, having tea parties and travelling... that was the plan, wasn't it? That's what was supposed to happen... now how am I supposed to live after death? The questions in my mind came fast and furious, but I didn't have too much time to think. Amazed at the report, people came from near and far to see Ros and confirm for themselves whether the report was true. We had more visitors in those next few days than we'd had in all the years we lived in that house. The flow of traffic was constant: some of the faces were familiar while others belonged to people I don't recall ever having met. I wanted to put an end to the traffic, but how unfair it would be to those who held his friendship so dear to them and who wanted to pay their respects before it was too late. To accommodate (and control) the crowd, the church decided that on December 15th, we would have Wednesday night prayer instead of our regularly-scheduled Bible study. That night, almost the entire church came together in our home and began to sing some of Ros' favorite songs.

He's sweet I know
He's sweet I know
Storm clouds may rise
Strong winds may blow
But I'll tell the world wherever I go
That I've found a savior, and he's sweet I know.

As the night wore on, an inexplicable calm filled the room as someone began to sing:

I feel like going on
I feel like going on
Though trials come on every hand
I feel like going on.

Everyone in the house that night knew that Ros Robertson's forty-five years on this earth was coming to an end, and it's as if each individual wanted to be a part of his final journey. Just as one song tapered down, someone else started to sing:

Jesus keeps me near the cross
There a precious fountain.
Free to all a healing stream
Flows from Calvary's mountain
In the cross, In the cross
Be my glory ever

Till my raptured soul shall find
Rest beyond river.
Near the cross I'll watch and wait
Hoping trusting ever
Till I reach the golden strand
Just beyond the river.

And when it seemed that the mood in the room was far too somber, the tempo changed with a more upbeat song:

By and by, when the morning comes;
When all the saints of God are gathered home,
We will tell the story how we've overcome
And we'll understand it better by and by.

Sing the wondrous love of Jesus;
Sing His mercy and His grace.
In the mansions bright and blessed,
He'll prepare for us a place.

When we all get to Heaven,
What a day of rejoicing that will be!
When we all see Jesus
We will sing and shout the victory.

While we walked the pilgrim pathway,
Clouds will overspread the sky;
But when traveling days are over
Not a shadow, not a sigh!

Let us then be true and faithful
Trusting, serving every day
Just one glimpse of him in glory
Wills the toils of life repay.

Onward to the prize before us
Soon His beauty we'll behold
Soon the pearly gates will open
We shall tread the streets of gold.

And then, I jumped in with Ros' favorite song. Years before he had told me how this song had been his mother's favorite. He would wake up many mornings with her singing this song, and it had become one of his favorites as well. I wanted him to hear it as he began his journey home.

I must needs go home
By the way of the cross
There's no other way but this:
I shall ne'er get sight of the gates of light
If the way of the cross I miss.

The way of the cross leads home,
The way of the cross leads home;
It's sweet to know as I onward go,
The way of the cross leads home.

I must needs go on in the blood-sprinkled way
The path that the Savior trod
If I ever climb to heights sublime,
Where the soul is at home with God.

Then I bid farewell to the way of the world,
To walk in it never more
For my Lord says "come", and I seek my home
Where He waits at the open door.

On December 16th, the day after that glorious prayer meeting, I noticed Ros did not get up as he had done the previous mornings. I went in to see what he needed, but he seemed unresponsive. I felt a bit guilty, thinking that maybe we had gone on too long the night before with our singing and praying, but the presence of the Lord was so wonderful and so palpable in the house that it was hard for us to come down off the high everyone felt. Still feeling a bit guilty, I decided to let him rest a bit longer and went about my day trying to take care of some household chores. However, by midday, there was still no response from him. I made some juices for his lunch and tried to get him to drink with a straw, but it seemed like he wasn't putting out any effort. I held his head in my arms, trying to encourage him to take even a sip of the juice, but as I looked in his eyes, I realized something was terribly wrong. There was no focus in his eyes; I saw nothing but the white of his eyes. I didn't have any kind of medical training, but I knew this could not be good. I gently laid him back down and dashed to the phone to call Annie the hospice nurse. It wasn't her day to visit, and of course, I didn't get a hold of her. I left her a frantic message indicating what the problem was and that she needed to call as soon as possible. In the meantime, the doorbell rang. I was so glad that someone else would be in the house beside me and my son, so I opened the door without bothering to look first. Standing there was Ros' boss and his plant manager who just happened to come by to see how he was doing. This was the worst possible time for their visit, but I could not turn them away since they had made the effort to see him. I took them to the room where Ros was lying, only to find him in a convulsive state as if he was having a full-body seizure. His eyes were totally rolled back, and his arms and legs were flailing involuntarily. Based on reports from the doctor and the hospice nurse, I figured this was the result of his organs shutting down, a reactionary movement as life slowly leaves the body. Hearing about the process was one thing, but seeing it play out live in front of me in my husband was more than I could bear. Clearly, it was also more than Ros' boss could bear. The frightened look on his boss's face told me that he could not leave the room fast enough. Telling me not to hesitate to call him if I needed anything, he and the plant manager cut their visit short and ran out the door, never to be seen again.

I looked around frantically for my son only to find him hiding in his room. He must have realized what was happening, and his self-preservation mechanism kicked in too. I wanted to join everyone and run away and hide from the sight in that room. Fear as I had never experienced before physically gripped me and did not want to let go. I had never witnessed anyone's death before, and seeing my husband make the transition from this life into eternity was not something I thought I would have to witness at this point in life. Instinctively, I reached for the phone to call for an ambulance when I remembered I had given Ros my word that he would not die in a hospital. Instead, I dialed the bishop's number and told him I believed Ros was dying, and I was scared to death. I don't know how long it was before he came; I only know that I was never so glad to see anyone in my entire life. How grateful I was that there was someone who could physically be there when I called. For several hours he sat with Ros, holding his hand and praying in that heavenly language. The house was filled with people as the word went out that Brother Robertson was leaving for home. Annie, the hospice nurse, finally made her way to the house. She came and took his pulse, confirming that it would not be long—his organs had completely shut down. Ros held on for several more hours, waiting I suspect, for his daughter to come home—she never made it in time. At 10:30 p.m. on December 16, 1999, Rosford Alvan Robertson left this world holding on to an earthly father as he was ushered into the arms of his Heavenly Father.

THEN I BID FAREWELL TO THE WAY OF THE
WORLD, TO WALK IN NEVER MORE; FOR MY
LORD SAYS, "COME," AND I SEEK MY HOME,
WHERE HE WAITS AT THE OPEN DOOR.

I was in the room adjoining his when my friend Deborah came in and ushered me to Ros' bedside. I walked in just in time to see him take his last breath. His hand was gripped tightly in Bishop's hands; so much so that when it was all over, the paramedics had to pry Ros' fingers out of the bishop's hand, one by one. Everyone recognized the smile on his face as he entered eternity—the journey was complete; home at last.

The days that followed Ros' death were extremely difficult for me, to say the least. The spirit of depression set in, and a loneliness I had never felt seemed to wrap me tightly in its hold. Trying to plan a funeral for a forty-five-year-old man was a very unnerving thing to do. Imagine walking into a funeral parlor to choose a suitable coffin for your husband—what exactly could be considered suitable? Does it really make a difference what the color of the box is or how comfortable it is inside? The best I can do in describing this feeling is to say it was a complete out-of-body experience. I was just a spectator to the whole scene, watching myself go through the motions. One moment I do recall so vividly was when someone sent flowers to the house. I thought I had made it clear that there should be no flowers coming to the house. Apparently, though, someone missed the memo and sent a bouquet to the house. I absolutely lost it. After all, flowers just reminded me of the fact that my husband was dead. And like him, those flowers would soon die, and I'd be the one responsible for disposing of the wasteful memento. Crazy as it might seem, the last thing I wanted was any kind of reminder of death.

I had chosen one tasteful spray of roses to be draped across Ros' coffin. As I entered the church that Tuesday morning after his death, it seemed like that bouquet of red roses was all I could focus on, as if turning my gaze to anything else would cause the arrangement to suddenly disappear. I kept watching the arrangement sitting neatly atop his closed burgundy coffin as someone held my hand, ushering me to the platform to sing a song. I wasn't sure I could do it, but I so wanted to give him one last song from me. During a brief recording career that tapered off during the course of our marriage, he had become my producer and sound engineer. Though he could not carry much of a note himself, he always encouraged my singing, saying he didn't have to sing himself to know what sounded good. I wanted desperately to sing him one last song.

When my life here is ended and I cross the swelling tide,
When the bright and glorious morning I shall see,

I shall know my redeemer when I reach the other side,
And His smile will be the first to welcome me.

Oh the soul-thrilling rapture when I see His blessed face
And the luster of his kindly beaming eyes;
How my poor heart will praise Him for the mercy love and grace
That prepares for me a mansion in the sky

I shall know Him, I shall know Him
And redeemed by His side I shall stand.
I shall know Him, I shall know Him
By the prints of the nails in His hand.

Thru the gates, thru the city in a robe of spotless white,
Jesus will lead me where no storm clouds ever fall,
In that glad song of ages, I shall mingle with delight
But I long to see my Jesus first of all.

I shall know Him, I shall know Him
And redeemed by His side I shall stand
I shall know Him, I shall know Him
By the prints of the nails in His hand.

The events of that day were overshadowed by my grief. I remember one of his sisters crying with such vehemence, and I sat there thinking, *Why is she grieving as one that has no hope?* It dawned on me that I could be doing the very same thing. Yes, I missed my husband; and yes, the days ahead seemed dark and dreary, but I remembered the Bible verse that warned about grieving as though we have no hope: there is a time to mourn and a time to cry, but the power of faith is knowing that, even if we cry now, we have an eternal assurance that those who die in Christ will also live with

Him. Even so, it was difficult to see that hope through the storm clouds that didn't want to leave me alone.

The church was overflowing with people. As we made our exit, we saw reams of people standing outside the sanctuary because there was not room on the inside to accommodate everyone. Seeing all those people who came to pay their last respects to a man who could no longer hear their words or feel their love, I wondered if he knew how much he was appreciated. Did these people, who came from near and far, take the time to tell him while he was with us how much they loved him? The words of an old James Cleveland song rang loud in my ears: *give me my flowers while I yet live so that I may see the beauty that they bring.* How many people in the crowd had taken time to let Ros see the beauty of their love? You know, maybe that's why I despised the flowers that were sent to the house—it seemed like a last attempt to make up for what should have been done for a person while they were still alive.

It was a cold and wet December day as the line of cars caravanned their way through the maze of city streets to the quiet, tree- lined cemetery just outside the city limits. As we made our way to the cemetery, I thought about how Ros wouldn't have liked the weather that day—it was too cold and too wet. Not realizing I was thinking out loud, someone in the car agreed with me, seconding the notion that Ros would not have liked that dreary day. The ride on the way to the cemetery seemed longer than it should have been. I had made the ride only a few days earlier when I went to choose his plot, but it did not seem as if the drive should have taken as long as it did that day. Then again, I failed to consider the pace of the procession. This was no ordinary ride—this was finality as we knew it on this earth. A man's body was being laid in its final resting place, closing one chapter here on earth, while another chapter opened in eternity. The finality of that ride made it drag on to no end, but then, no sooner did we arrive at the cemetery, it was time to leave. I knew the choir had sung at the church, and the pastors had given their comments, and the eulogy was rendered, but when we got to the gravesite, it seemed like everything moved too quickly. Maybe it was in an effort to stop time, or maybe it was just because I didn't know what else to do; but whatever the reason, I stopped at Ros' graveside to sing him one last song to let him know that I could never and would never forget who he was and what he meant to this family.

Till we meet
Till we meet
Till we meet at Jesus' feet;
Till we meet
Till we meet
God be with you till we meet again.

I would have sung at his graveside all day long if someone hadn't forcibly taken me by the arm to lead me back to the waiting car. I kept looking back as I was led to the car, noticing that the coffin was still sitting on the belt. My brother-in-law informed me a week later that he waited along with his nephew to make sure the cemetery workers lowered and covered the casket. Somehow, that thought brought a strange peace, and I was most grateful for it.

The days following Ros' service were unbearable. The spirits of depression and fear had such a strong hold on me that I could not seem to shake myself free from their death grips. My mind had so many different internal conversations that at times, I struggled to distinguish between reality and fantasy. The biggest hurdle to get over was whether or not God had failed me. So many people had prayed, believing that we would see a miracle. We asked without wavering, believing we would get what we asked for, never doubting that God was able to heal my husband—how, then, was it that we did not see what we had prayed for? While I contemplated this question in my mind, the phone rang and brought me back to reality: it was Deborah calling, letting me know she wanted to talk with me. She said she had something to tell me, but she could not share it until she believed I was ready to hear it. So on December 22nd, a week after Ros' death, Deborah and I met at a local restaurant. It was so good to get out of the house. Most of my visiting family members had already left, supposedly intending for me to get back to a normal routine—but what exactly could be considered normal after you just lost your spouse? Either way, I was glad to meet her just to be out of my house for a while. As we sat down and ordered, she was so overcome by emotions she could hardly contain herself. She mentioned that she wanted to tell me something the very night that it happened, but just knew it was not the right time to tell me such a thing. Then, she began her story:

> "The night Brother Ros was leaving us, I sat in your living room, and I saw what I have never seen before and perhaps will never see again in my lifetime.
>
> There were ministering ANGELS that went from your room to his room all the while until he made the transition. Back and forth they went with absolute precision, as soldiers that were given specific orders by Heaven's Creator."

Tears rolled down her face as she related the story; then she said something that really threw me for a loop. She went on to tell me how much God must love me that he would send angels to serve me in my greatest time of need. What do you say to a person who says God loves you so much that he gave angels specific orders to leave the courts of Heaven to go to a young widow to help her make that transition? The rivers of tears flowed from my eyes in that small restaurant. In my prayer, the Tuesday morning before Ros died, after he announced that he was ready to go home, I had prayed and asked the LORD to send His angels to escort him home and to let me know, some way, somehow, that the angels had indeed come for him. Deborah could not have known what I prayed in my private time that morning, but my Heavenly Father heard my prayer. Not only did he hear my prayer, but he answered, sending an earthly angel to let me know that my petition was granted. I had just fought a battle with myself wondering if God failed us, only to find out that not only did He not fail me, but He had a plan in place to help me through the difficult times that would come. At that moment in time, I remembered Ros' visions—the elderly lady in the chair, the family building the fence—and it all started to make sense. All the while, angels were surrounding not only him, but our family, building that hedge of protection that our friends and family had also prayed for. Still thinking about Deborah's story when I walked back through the door of my house, Jordan greeted me with a great big hug. Before I could even mention anything about my encounter, my son started telling me about what he saw the night his father died. Dumbfounded, I listened in amazement as my eight-year-old child confirmed that, indeed, God hadn't forgotten us and had answered our prayer, not the way we wanted, but the way we needed. Ros was ready to go home to glory and went with a smile, knowing that the God in whom he put his faith and trust had sent heavenly messengers to take care of his family, ensuring they would all be okay.

The purpose of this book is twofold: First, to let the world know that a very special man by the name of Rosford Alvan Robertson once lived, and I had the privilege and the honor of being his wife. He was not a great inventor: he did not discover any new worlds, nor did he solve the problems of the world, but he made his world a better place by living and walking according to the principles of God's word. He was a faithful husband and father, a loving son, a brother, and a caring uncle; but the most important and most enduring role he played was as a servant of the MOST HIGH GOD. He lived in obedience, and once he found the joy of serving Christ, he dedicated his life to telling others about the Good News of Jesus Christ. The legacy he left of prayer and dedication to the things of God will not soon be forgotten. Ros made a difference in the lives of those who knew him. He was passionate about the things of GOD and had a love for people's souls, a love that would compel him to get in his car and drive around the city to pray that people would realize how much GOD loves each and every one of us, made in his own image. That same passion drove him to his knees in the wee hours of his mornings, petitioning the throne of Heaven for an answer on behalf of others in need. When his Heavenly Father saw that his purpose on earth was fulfilled, He called him home. Because Ros' desire was always to obey his Lord, he responded in absolute obedience and went home.

The second purpose of this book is to speak words of wisdom to those who have faced sickness and the loss of a loved one such as my children and I have. Even though it was confirmed that the Lord had a plan for us and sent heavenly messengers to help, it still didn't make living with the reality of this flesh easy. We often despise our struggles simply because we don't understand why the LORD would allow us to go through such difficult times. I have come to understand, though, that everything God allows in our lives is for a purpose. He does nothing without a plan in place, but all things work together for good to them that love God and who are the called according to His purpose (Romans 8:28). For me, the greatest lesson in all this was to put my faith, not in the wisdom of men but in the power of who God is (1 Corinthians 2:5). Before all of this came into play, my life revolved around my family: my children had to have the best education money could buy, my husband had to have the best job—in my mind, that was the only way we were going to get ahead in life. We had to be on top of our game for our plan to work out for us. But in all of my planning, I didn't make room for Almighty God. As I look back over those years, I realized he was waving the proverbial red flag saying, *I am here but where are you? In your self-sufficiency, is there any room for me? You seem to be doing all the right things: you go to church on Sundays and prayer meetings on Saturdays; you make sure the children are well-dressed for Sunday school; your tithes and offering are intact; but what kind of relationship do you and I have? Am I your first choice when something goes wrong, or am I just a convenient alternative in case nothing else works?* I had been saying with my mouth that this church business was really all about building a relationship with Jesus Christ, but where did I stand in my relationship with Him?

If you are going through struggles in your life, perhaps it's God's way of waiving that proverbial red flag in your life: DON'T IGNORE IT God is a GOD of absolute grace—His Word declares that His grace is sufficient for every need in our lives. When I first realized Ros was ill, instead of looking to the all-sufficient One, the first thing I did was put on my "fix it" hat. We had our share of difficulties before, and this was just another problem for which there had to be a solution. But when I could not make this problem go away, I made it God's problem—clearly—He had failed us because I prayed and believed but still didn't see a miracle, forgetting that His ways were not my ways. When I had tried everything else and everything else failed, I tried God as an afterthought. When He did not respond as I thought He should, the war between my faith and my flesh waged in the battlefield of my mind. Questions of whether or not God really loved me surfaced. I knew He did love me, but the reality of His love and the pain I felt seemed two polar opposites that could not... would not reconcile in my mind.

It took me years after Ros' death to realize my life still had a purpose. With the clouds of depression and loneliness still trying to cloud my mind, I decided it was time to change. The only way I knew how to really change was by immersing myself in reading the Bible. I started by doing a study on the life of John the Baptist. While visiting my now ailing mother (who had since moved back to Montreal with Nicole after Nicole graduated from Lehigh), I had a chance to spend some quiet time in Nicole's apartment. As I sat down at the kitchen table with my coffee to continue this study on the life of John, a burning question kept coming to the forefront of my mind: knowing John's impending fate, why did Jesus do nothing when his cousin was in prison? He must have been concerned—after all, John was family, and when family is in trouble, the first thing you do is rush to their aid. Yet, nowhere in the book of John does it indicate that Jesus did anything when he was told his cousin was in prison. My curiosity got the best of me, so I did what the Bible says I should do—*I asked* (James 1:5). The spirit of the LORD spoke in no uncertain terms: *John knew what his purpose was.* John the Baptist was born for no other reason but to point the way to the One who *is* the way. There are times when you receive a revelation and you question whether or not it was from God. This time, my relationship with God had grown to the point where there was no question—I knew His voice in the way I recognized my children's voices, and in that morning, I knew with every fiber of my being that the Holy Spirit had spoken. Once your purpose here on earth is fulfilled, there is no point in hanging around. That's why John could say with such confidence, *He must increase, but I must decrease* (John 3:30). Ros fulfilled his purpose to declare the greatness of Almighty God and to teach his family and others to do the same; once that was done, there was no reason for him to hang around in spite of the heartache that brought to his family and friends. A purposeful life is one that is ordained by the ALMIGHTY, and one that succeeds by accomplishing that which it was born to do.

ABOUT THE AUTHOR

Joy Robertson represents the strength that we find in many single mothers who have raised doctors, lawyers, athletes, and many entertainers. Based in Waterbury, Connecticut, she represents countless women who have life's odds stacked against them. She was born in Jamaica and raised by a single mother. As a teenager, she moved to Canada as a talented vocalist to pursue a better life. There she met Rosford Robertson, her husband-to-be.

Soon, they were married and relocated to Connecticut in 1990. They had a son and a daughter. The family was healthy, happy, and thriving. Nine years later, tragedy hit as their family found out Rosford was diagnosed with cancer. This was a crushing blow seeing how they had one child entering a critical development stage in his life and another child in her first year of college. About ten months later, the family lost Rosford, and Joy was forced to support a college student, keep a mortgage, and raise an unruly adolescent on her own. Through much prayer and divine supernatural help, Joy was able to navigate her way through this dark time, helping her daughter graduate and keeping her son from becoming another statistic in our country. Joy's story is one that any parent and spouse can relate to. Not only does it keep you hooked from start to finish, but it leaves you with a sense of hope when everything around you says it's hopeless. It is truly a testament of God's love and grace toward his children.

Written by: Jordan Phillip Robertson

www.ingramcontent.com/pod-product-compliance
Lightning Source LLC
Chambersburg PA
CBHW020332130626
46549CB00003B/1132

* 9 781965 687581 *